UNDERSTANDING THE TIMES

INTERPRETING GOD'S PLAN FOR THE ENDTIMES CHURCH

UNDERSTANDING THE TIMES

INTERPRETING GOD'S PLAN FOR THE ENDTIMES CHURCH

E. C. NAKELI, PH.D.

© 2017 by E.C. Nakeli

King's Word Publishing, 2016

For your questions and publishing needs, write to:

    E.C. Nakeli
Christian Missionary Fellowship International
40 S Church st
Westminster, MD 21157
E-mail: *ecnakeli@yahoo.com*

Printed in the United States of America

All rights reserved. No part of this publication may be reproduced, stored in a retrieval systems, or transmitted in any form or by any means — for example, electronic, photocopy, recording — without the prior written permission of the publisher. The only exception is brief quotations in printed reviews.

E.C. Nakeli

To contact the author, write to:

    E.C. Nakeli
40 S Church st
Westminster, MD 21157
E-mail: *ecnakeli@yahoo.com*

Understanding The Times/ E.C. Nakeli

ISBN: 978-1-945055-07-2

Unless otherwise indicated, Scriptures references are from

    THE HOLY BIBLE, NEW INTERNATIONAL VERSION®, NIV®
Copyright © 1973, 1978, 1984, 2011 by Biblica, Inc™
  Used by permission. All rights reserved worldwide.

Table of Contents

PREFACE vi
CHAPTER ONE 7
THE TIMES WE LIVE IN 7
   THE NEED 8
   THE ENEMY KNOWS IT 9
   ARE THERE SOME WISE HEARTS OUT THERE? 10
CHAPTER TWO 14
THE URGENCY IN WHICH WE LIVE 14
   THE PROBLEM 15
   REDEEMING THE TIME 17
      YOUR RELATIONSHIPS: 19
      YOUR EMOTIONS: 20
      YOUR VOCATION 21
      YOUR POSSESSIONS: 22
      TAKING STOCK 24
CHAPTER THREE 26
THE PRESENT TIME 26
   IT IS TIME TO WAKE UP 27
   WHY MUST YOU WAKE UP? 27
      To Engage In Battle 27
      To Behold His Face and Glory 29
      To Regain The Authentic Vision 29
   THE NIGHT IS ALMOST OVER: 31
   THE DAY IS ALMOST HERE: 32
      Putting Aside Deeds Of Darkness 32
      Putting On The Armor of Light 33
CHAPTER FOUR 34
A TIME TO CONFRONT REALITY-1 34
   A WRETCHED CHURCH 35
   A PITIFUL CHURCH 37
   A POOR CHURCH 39
      WE ARE POOR IN POWER: 39
      WE ARE POOR IN FAITH 40
      WE ARE POOR IN LOVE: 41

LET'S GET PRACTICAL	42
WE ARE POOR IN PRAISE AND WORSHIP	43
WE ARE POOR IN BLESSINGS:	45
A BLIND CHURCH:	46
A NAKED CHURCH	47
CHAPTER FIVE	49
A TIME TO CONFRONT REALITY -2	49
A DEFEATED CHURCH	49
SEVEN MANIFESTATIONS OF DIVISION	50
1. DISCRIMINATION:	50
2. DESPISE:	52
3. DISRESPECT:	53
4. DISREGARD:	54
5. DISTRUST:	55
6. DUPLICITY:	55
7. DEFEAT:	57
WE MUST IDENTIFY AND CONFRONT THE ACHANS	57
Are there some mourners?	61
Reasons why we cannot stand	62
CHAPTER SIX	65
A TIME TO CONFRONT REALITY-3	65
A LEPROUS CHURCH	65
HAVE WE LOST OUR SALTINESS?	68
CHAPTER SEVEN	70
A TIME TO REBUILD THE FOUNDATIONS	70
A DIVINE PRINCIPLE	73
DO YOU HAVE A FOUNDATION?	74
WHAT IS YOUR FOUNDATION MADE OF?	75
CHAPTER EIGHT	81
A TIME TO RUBUILD THE FOUNDATIONS-2	81
WHAT IS THE STATE (CONDITION) OF YOUR FOUNDATION?	81
Guard your heart	84
THE HARD REALITY	85
Foundations first!	87
WHERE TO START	88
WHAT HAPPENS WHEN THE FOUNDATIONS ARE REBUILT?	90

- CHAPTER NINE 92
- OUR RESPONSE 92
  - A TIME TO SEEK THE LORD 92
  - HOW DO WE SEEK HIM? 94
  - WHY MUST WE RETURN? 95
    - FOR REVIVAL: 96
    - FOR RESTORATION 103
- CHAPTER TEN 105
- A TIME FOR DISTINCTION 105
  - GOD'S COMMITMENT: 107
  - SEPARATING THE RANKS 108
  - WHAT BLOCKS VISION? 109
  - A CALL TO THE MOUNTAIN 112
    - MOUNTAIN TOP IS YOUR HOME 115
    - OVERCOME YOUR FEARS 117
- CHAPTER ELEVEN 122
- A TIME TO LIVE READY 122
  - LIVING READY IMPLIES SELF-EXAMINATION 122
  - LIVING READY MEANS LIVING HOLY 125
  - DISCONNECT THE SUPPLY 128
- CHAPTER TWELVE 129
- A TIME TO CROSS JORDAN 129
  1. The Israelites set out from Shittim to Jordan. 132
  2. The Priests had to take up their responsibility: 137
  3. The people had to move out of position: 138
  4. They had to follow the Ark 139
  5. They were to keep a distance between them and the ark. 143
  6. The People Had To Consecrate Themselves: 143
  7. The Priests had to Demonstrate Faith, Boldness and Sacrifice: 144
- CHAPTER THIRTEEN 145
- A TIME TO GIVE BIRTH 145
  - Make Room! 147
  - A Time for Enlargement 150
- CHAPTER FOURTEEN 152
- A TIME FOR THE GLORY TO RETURN 152
  - It Is High Time We Opened the Door to the King 156

PREFACE

I began writing this book in the fall of 2006, took a long break from writing due to other time constraints and returned to completing the book in the summer of 2009. Although this book was completed several years back, it is only now I feel the strong conviction to have it released. Two main reasons why I feel the urgency: first, the state of the global church and world affairs reflect almost perfectly, what is described in this book, second we are running out of time as the hand of the clock ticks towards the close of time.

I send this book out with the faith that, the Holy Spirit will put it into the right hands, of people who will mobilize others to maximize the final minutes of the time allotted this generation.

CHAPTER ONE

THE TIMES WE LIVE IN

In every event, in every game, in every conflict, in every ceremony, no matter the length of time it takes, some moments are more solemn and crucial to the final outcome than others. What happens within those defining moments is of utmost importance to the parties involved. Those who are to make any significant contribution to the success of the event must have engraved in their minds the crucial nature of such defining moments. Whether it is in a game, a ceremony, a conflict, a relationship or anything else, we must seek to understand how close we are to its defining moment.

The Christian life is a race we are called to run, a relationship we are called to keep, and a battle we are called to fight. The outcome of each face of the Christian life will affect the final results of how we have lived our lives. Many people seem to be oblivious to interpreting the signs of the times. It seems that very few who bear His Name have understood that the times in which this generation is living are of vital importance to the King and His Kingdom. If the church must fulfill her calling to be the salt of the earth and the light of the world, she just must come to grips with the fact that she has far less time than she thinks.

Let every Christian folk across this terrestrial ball see the need to understand the times. If not, we shall awaken to realize that the night is long past and the day has been wasted. Can we afford to allow ourselves to drift in the wrong direction? Can we allow the time to pass by with the task given us still standing as though it will take eternity to accomplish? Are we accusing the Master of demanding too much of us? Do we claim that He left us with an impossible task to accomplish? If we need to wake up then it is now, before the curtains are drawn. It seems to me that they are halfway drawn, and in a matter of seconds, it will be over.

THE NEED

When, thousands of years ago, long before the birth of the church, Solomon out of wisdom wrote, "There is a time for everything, and a season for every activity under heaven" (Eccl 3:1), he meant just that. Everything has a time frame within which it must be done. Every activity has a season within which its outcome is determined, within which maximum impact must be registered, and after which the extent of its impact can only be minimal. The King James Version puts it this way, "To everything there is a season, and a time to every purpose under heaven."

This is the time for the church to accomplish her purpose. This is the time for the church to make her maximum impact before the King's return. More than ever, it is the time to make an all-out attack on the enemy. Now, more than ever, is the time to lay all on the altar of the Gospel. More than ever, it is the time to judge everything on the basis of its impact in promoting the Gospel and edifying the church.

This is the time for every Christian, irrespective of his physical or spiritual age, to discover his calling and use it effectively "to prepare God's people for the works of service, so that the body of Christ may be built up until we all reach unity in faith and <u>in the knowledge of the Son of God</u> and <u>become mature</u>, attaining to the whole measure of the fullness of Christ." (Eph 4:12-13).

Is it not time for the barriers of doctrine and denominationalism to fall? Is it not time for Gospel Ministers to keep away their differences? Is it not time for us to abandon our own ideologies and return to the word of God? Without these can we ever "reach unity in faith"? Can we really get the people of God prepared for the service they must carry out within these last days?

Are you exploring and exploiting new effective ways to increase your knowledge of the Son? Are you spending maximum time in quiet meditation on His word? Are you spending maximum time to read and study the Word? Are you spending maximum time praying and listening to the voice of the Shepherd? If not how do you expect to become mature in your faith? Are our churches not made up mostly of spiritual dwarfs and babies?

Do we expect to attain "the whole measure of the fullness of Christ" through such superficial commitment to the Gospel's course manifested in the lack of the spirit of sacrifice? We must "go on to maturity" if we must fulfill our commission. May the shepherds of God's flock get everyone involved in the movement to maturity!

THE ENEMY KNOWS IT

"Therefore rejoice you heavens and you who dwell in them! But woe to the earth and the sea, because the devil has gone down to you! He is filled with fury, because he knows that his time is short."(Rev 12:12)

It seems to me that the devil has understood the urgency of the present time more than the church. If there have been woes and distresses on earth it has never been in such a great magnitude as it is today. Anarchy and lawlessness are at their highest levels. Many more nations are in a state of civil strife than has ever been. Global terrorism is on the rise, the threat of a nuclear holocaust due to nuclear proliferation is stronger today than even in the days of the cold war. In spite of the promise of health for all by the year 2000, which is long past, there is a high spread of diseases in most parts of the world.

Poverty and hunger seem to be on a steady rise. Natural disasters are more frequent than has ever been in human history. Why? Because the devil "knows that his time is short" and therefore seeks to cause maximum harm to God's beloved human race before he is taken captive. The Bible says "He knows ...", and if I may emphasis, I would say "He knows that he knows that he knows ..." Once a man knows something, his whole life is affected by it.

The Greek word used here for "knows", eidō, has in it knowledge which results from having seen and experienced. The devil has seen and experienced from the battles in the heavens that his time is short. The sad thing is that he seems to understand it more than us, the church, and he takes advantage of this shameful and avoidable ignorance.

ARE THERE SOME WISE HEARTS OUT THERE?

"… and the wise heart will know the proper time and procedure. For there is a proper time and procedure for every matter …" (Eccl 8:5^b-6^a).

It takes nothing but wisdom to know the urgency of the time we live in. Such wisdom is not carnal, but is imparted by the Spirit of God in the hearts of those who earnestly long to make maximum impact for the kingdom. If there is a proper time to invest everything possible, to take any risk for the Gospel cause, to lay down our lives that others may live, it is now.

The wise heart will be led into effective procedures that lead to maximum investment of time, energy, relationships, talents and other valuable resources. Certainly there are some who have understood the times, but this is only a small negligible fraction compared to the total number of those who bear His Name. This however should not be the case.

From the above verses, two aspects emerge and define two sets of people. Let us bring out the points and the categories of people will automatically be seen.
(i) There is a proper time
(ii) There is a proper procedure

In the church today there are people who know the proper time but not the proper procedure, and those who know the proper procedure but not the proper time. However there are a few, the wise hearts, who know and understand both the proper time and the proper procedure. It is the more reason why ministers of the Gospel must seek to enhance mutual cooperation, so that those who understand the times come together with those who understand the procedure, for effective and maximum impact.

In the Old Testament, there was a group of people who understood both the times and the procedure. When Saul, King of Israel died, many warriors came in large numbers to join David at Hebron. Amongst them were the "men of Issachar, who understood the times and knew what Israel should do…" (1 Chro 12:32). These men understood both the proper time and the proper procedure (course) Israel had to take to ensure peace and a smooth transition. The church is in greater need of such men and women today. May God raise such people in great numbers across the nations. Then the world will be turned right side-up in the shortest period of time.

But does the tribe from which these men came mean anything? I believe strongly it does. They were men from the tribe of Issachar which means reward. If you remember how Issachar the father of the tribe came to existence, then it will be clear why it was men from "Issachar who understood the times and knew what Israel should do". Issachar was conceived by Leah, wife of Jacob, because she decided to sacrifice something (see Gen 30:14-18). Issachar was the reward of Leah's sacrifice of her mandrakes. She gave her mandrakes in order to bring forth Issachar.

> *If there is a proper time to invest everything possible, to take any risk for the Gospel cause, to lay down our lives that others may live, it is now.*

I believe the church is in great lack of men and women of such virtue who understand the times because she is made up mostly of men and women who have refused to sacrifice anything for the Gospel. The cross life seems to be as far removed from such as the east is from the west. The wise heart can only come as a result of sacrifice: sacrifice of personal goals and interests, personal comfort and ease; sacrifice of the building of personal kingdoms and empires; sacrifice of that which is precious to us for the welfare of others. What would all this mean practically?

It may mean cutting down expenditures where possible for the sake of giving more to missions or helping someone else in a more serious need than yours. It may mean making room in your house, in your finances and other resources so that someone else might be accommodated. These are the kinds of sacrifices, little or great, we must all engage in if we must understand the times we live in.

Above all, we must respond to the command, "in view of God's mercy to offer your bodies as living sacrifices, holy and pleasing to God" (Romans 12:1). When we do this, we shall be able to respond wholeheartedly to the injunction "Do not conform any longer to the pattern of this world, but be transformed by the renewing of your mind. Then you will be able to test and approve what God's will is-- his good, pleasing and perfect will" (Rom 12:2). Unless there is this sacrifice, there can be no transformation, and unless there is transformation we cannot understand the urgency of the times we live in.

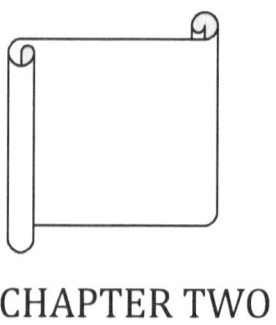

CHAPTER TWO

THE URGENCY IN WHICH WE LIVE

The times in which we are living seem to be added time. That which must be done now, if not accomplished will be lost and lost forever. The urgency of the hour cannot be overemphasized. May the good Lord out of His infinite grace and mercy sharpen our spiritual sensitivity so that we become totally discerning of what is being prepared in the spiritual. May those whom God has raised and established in the office of prophets, teachers and shepherds sound it unequivocally, again and again, that it is time to do all that must be done. It is time to shift from planning to action, from dreams to realities. It is time to raise the alarm for all to hear and respond accordingly.

Shall we dare to say that the leaders of today have failed the church? Shall we dare to say more and more people are being deceived to join the trend of materialistic and self-indulgent living through many a sermon preached and many a conference organized? Where are the sermons which sound the call to the way of the cross? Where are the sermons which point to self-effacing, self-abasing, self-sacrificial service to the King and His Kingdom? Where are the conferences to train young men and women for voluntary Christian service? Where are the preachers, who like prophet Micah would shout out, "But as for me, I am filled with power, with the Spirit of the LORD, and with justice and might, to declare to Jacob his transgression, to Israel his sin" (Mic 3:8)?

Have we not spent our time pointing at the world's sins while condoning with these same sins within the church of the First Born? Do we dare to say many today are afraid to confront the church with her sins, her backsliding and her compromise? *O Lord, raise people filled with Your power, Your might, Your Justice, and above all Your Spirit to declare without reservation or fear of being misunderstood or rejected, the sins of professing Christians.*

> *Where are the sermons which sound the call to the way of the cross? Where are the sermons which point to self-effacing, self-abasing, self-sacrificial service to the King and His Kingdom? Where are the conferences to train young men and women for voluntary Christian service?*

THE PROBLEM

The greatest problem the church faces today is that her leaders have failed to interpret the signs of the time. They seem to be given over to the interpretation of many other things than they are to interpreting the time in the Spirit. More than two thousand years ago the Lord Jesus found the same failure with the religious leaders of His day.

"The Pharisees and Sadducees came to Jesus and tested him by asking him to show them a sign from heaven. He replied, "When evening comes, you say, `It will be fair weather, for the sky is red,' and in the morning, `Today it will be stormy, for the sky is red and

overcast.' You know how to interpret the appearance of the sky, but you cannot interpret the signs of the times"(Matt 16:1-3).

The signs seem to be everywhere for anyone to discern and perceive the closeness in which we are to the Lord's return. Many have failed to interpret the signs of the times to those they are leading; people seem to major in the non-essentials, reason for the indulgence we see all around Christian circles. This is the problem: those called to interpret the signs of the times are busy prophesying "much wine and corn" to the people. "Business as usual" is the order of the day. Let me sound a warning, as I sense in my spirit, *"Hear this, you leaders of the house of Jacob, you rulers of the house of Israel, who despise justice and distort all that is right; who build Zion with bloodshed, and Jerusalem with wickedness. Her leaders judge for a bribe, her priests teach for a price, and her prophets tell fortunes for money. Yet they lean upon the LORD and say, "Is not the LORD among us? No disaster will come upon us." Therefore because of you, Zion will be plowed like a field, Jerusalem will become a heap of rubble, the temple hill a mound overgrown with thickets"* (Mic 3:9-12).

Are we not building personal empires at the price of the blood of men who could be reached with the Gospel? Can't we see that there are more fortune-tellers all around Christian circles today than there are prophets of God? Yeah, they prophesy so as to impress the people for the sake of their offerings? It seems to me that these fortune-tellers are encouraged by the very people who listen to them. As in the days of Micah, "if a liar and deceiver comes and says, I will prophesy for you plenty of wine and beer; he would be just the prophet for this people!"(Mic 2:11).

Of these fortune-tellers the Lord says, "But if they had stood in my council, they would have proclaimed my words to my people and would have turned them from their evil ways and from their evil deeds" (Jer 23:22). Where are the sermons that point out to the people their sin and the way out? Where are the sermons to rebuke the compromise that has overshadowed the demarcation between the carnal and the spiritual, the world and the church, the unsaved and the saved, the pretender and the sincere, the fake and the genuine?

Let us return to the message of the cross, let us show people the need for sacrifice, the need to die to self, die to sin, die to the world; its gains, its luxuries, its comfort, its praise and admiration. Let us preach the need for total consecration or nothing, the need for sanctification, the readiness to meet the King. That is what we need now!

> *To redeem the time, you too must know and understand the musts of your life and labor to concentrate on them.*

REDEEMING THE TIME

"Redeeming the time because the days are evil" (Eph 5:16, KJV).

The Greek word used here for redeem is ēxa gŏrazō, a composition of two other words. It means to buy up or to ransom. It is as though you go to a market square, give out something in exchange for time.

How can we as Christians, having understood the urgency of the time, work as to redeem the time? What can we give up in exchange for the time we so badly need? To redeem time, we must look at the non-essentials in our daily schedule and trim off most of the time that is allocated to them. We must reduce the non-essentials to the least in order to invest that time in what is really needed.

Since we are called to "be imitators of God" (Eph 5:1), let us look at some of the musts of the life of God incarnate, the Lord Jesus Christ; these are some of the musts of His life (all from KJV)

- Suffer many things Mk 8:31
- Be rejected Mk 9:12
- Be about His Father's business Lk 2:49
- Preach the kingdom of God Lk 4:43
- The scripture must be fulfilled in Him Lk 22:37
- Handed over to sinners Lk 24:7
- Be lifted up Jn 3:14
- Work the works of Him that sent Him Jn 9:4
- Rise again from the death Jn 20:9

To redeem the time, you too must know and understand the musts of your life and labor to concentrate on them. We said before that redeeming the time will imply giving up something in exchange, not only the non-essentials but also maximizing the time we spend on what we must do.

> *"What I mean, brothers, is that the time is short. From now on those who have wives should live as if they had none; those who mourn, as if they did not; those who are happy, as if they were not; those who buy something, as if it were not theirs to keep; those who use the things of the world, as if not engrossed in them. For this world in its present form is passing away"*(I Cor 7:29-31).

The above passage is a call to maximize our time, and how to redeem time by being watchful over the things we engage ourselves in. Let us see some aspects from the passage which must be handled with care and tact.

YOUR RELATIONSHIPS:

Paul focused on the marriage relationship as one of the things which we must handle with care and wisdom. However, we can draw a generalization for all other relationships. We must ensure that our commitment to them does not interfere with our commitment to the Lord. When getting into any relationship, the question that must be asked is, "How does, or how will this relationship enable me concentrate on the musts of my life?" or "How will this relationship enable the other party accomplish the musts of his or her life?"

We must seek to understand whether the relationship will be healthy spiritually, emotionally, financially, psychologically and socially. If such a relationship will not work for the welfare of both parties then it is not worth it. Relationships should be evaluated on the basis of whether they enhance the accomplishment of God's call on the lives of those involved and consequently, the fulfillment of destinies.

In this light will you be honest to re-evaluate the usefulness of your relationships? Have you until now, attached great importance to unhealthy relationships? Will you from this moment attach more importance to your determinant relationships? You can redeem time by breaking unhealthy relationships, that is, those which will ultimately at best take you or the other party to nowhere and at worst shipwreck your destinies. Such relationships usually do not have a defined purpose from the very beginning and lead only to time wastage. Run away from any relationship that prevents total commitment and consecration to God.

Even for those relationships which are essential, do not give more time than is absolutely necessary for the spiritual, emotional, psychological and social welfare of every party involved. That is why Paul says, "Those who have wives should live as if they had none." This is not to say you should keep away from your responsibility, but that do not allow marriage to cause you to lose focus of your call to please the Lord. "I am saying this for your own good, not to restrict you, but that you may live the right way in undivided devotion to the Lord" (I Cor 7:35). You cannot afford to sacrifice devotion to God on the altar of any relationship.

> *If such a relationship will not work for the welfare of both parties then it is not worth it. Relationships should be evaluated on the basis of whether they enhance the accomplishment of God's call on the lives of those involved and consequently, the fulfillment of destinies.*

YOUR EMOTIONS:

Our emotions greatly affect our use of time and other associated resources. The way a man feels at any one time determines what he does and how he does it. Thus, most often our feelings determine our output even when we do not allow them to express themselves outwardly. You may suppress your emotions whether positive or negative but you cannot suppress their effects. That is why we must not only labor to have self-control, but we must allow the Spirit of God to take absolute control over our emotions, be they emotions of disapproval or emotions of approval, negative or positive emotions.

When we allow the Spirit to take absolute control of our emotions, He expresses His own emotions through us. Whatever the case, we must be in control of our emotions and not the emotions controlling us. That is why Paul could say, "those who mourn, as if they did not; those who are happy as if they were not." Have you lost a loved one? Do not allow that to cause you to lose focus and devotion. Are you happy and celebrating? Do not allow your happiness to distract you from your devotion to Christ.

YOUR VOCATION

The choice of vocation greatly affects and determines one's devotion to the Lord. It is true that we should do everything as unto the Lord. But this does not cancel the effect one's vocation has on his or her devotion to God and to the course of the Gospel of Christ Jesus. Your calling should determine your vocation. If you have known your calling you must choose a vocation which will give you ample time to exercise and fulfill your calling.

Several years ago I was offered a better Job, though still in the teaching field but which required more of my time. It is true that I was going to be better placed financially, be opened to a higher level of society and enjoy many other advantages of teaching in an International School in the largest city of my home country. But after carefully evaluating its effect on my calling, I decided to turn down the offer.

This was a matter of priority. It was exchanging a higher standard of living for more time to invest in my calling, especially in the writing of Christian Literature. I cannot recall the numerous times close friends and relatives have expressed their wish that I get something better, knowing my potentials but I have decided to stay where I am, doing what I am doing until the proper time comes.

On what basis did you choose your vocation? On the basis of the impact you will create in the building of God's kingdom or on the basis of the luxury it will provide? I have a friend who works in the financial sector. I have watched him dedicate more and more time to his job at the detriment of his Christian responsibilities. I have watched another brother give more time to his business at the price of his availability for the services he rendered in church.

The things you own are not neutral; they affect your walk with God positively or negatively depending on your attitude and attachment to them.

I know there are people called to the market place. If that is your calling, then put in your all to produce the best results. But never let it be at the price of a fruitful personal relationship with the Savior. Do not allow your job to consume all the vital part of your day so that you have little or nothing left to offer your God.

YOUR POSSESSIONS:

What a man possesses is not neutral. One's possessions either increase his level of devotion to God, decrease it, or cause him not to be devoted at all. There are people who, over the years, have refused to possess certain things, not because the things are evil or sinful but because such things will not help them to maximize their time and devotion to God. One of the world's most renowned architects has denied himself many things so he can devote more time to his work. He has no cell phone, does not visit the internet, and does not watch TV etc. All this is so that he can have fewer distractions from people around.

It is clear that there are things which if one refuses to possess will not affect one's life in anyway. In this case there are no rules. Each one should be able to determine with respect to his calling and vocation the things that act as a distraction or time waster. Will you mind carrying out an inventory of your possessions? Will you mark an X on those which are not absolute necessities but consume your time, attention, finances, emotions etc.? Will you dispose of all such things? You can put them on sale or make gifts to those who absolutely need them. What you keep is never neutral. It will either propel you along the path to maximizing your time and potentials or cause you to waste them.

A man's thoughts will always be affected by his possessions. The more you possess the more reason to worry about. Besides it is not only what a man possesses that matters but his attitude to it. "Those who buy something, as if it were not theirs to keep" means that we should not have our minds attached to what we possess. Our lives should not be affected to any extent by our possessions. Live with the mind to let go what you must let go.

Do not have a possessive attitude towards things for this will render you ineffective in many areas of your life. It will affect your spiritual and social input and consequently your output. Thus our level of spiritual maturity and consecration greatly determines our attitude towards possessions. One man may own many things without any attachment to them because of his level of consecration and separation unto God while another may own just a few things yet has his whole life attached to them.

Thus, we cannot judge people by their possessions but by their attitudes towards what they own. For example, one man may absent himself from the prayer night because he is afraid thieves will break in and steal from his house while he is away. Another will not attend meetings out of town because he is afraid the children will be careless with his possessions, no matter the quantity. Another man may own many things, yet this does not keep him away from a prayer night or any service that requires his being away from home for some time. He allows God to keep watch over his things because he has come to understand that "unless the Lord watches over a city the watchmen stand guard in vain" (Ps 127).

TAKING STOCK

"Those who use the things of this world, as if not engrossed on them"

The King James Version of that verse reads "And they that use this world, as not abusing it". The Greek word used for abuse here is Katachŏamai which means to overuse i.e. to misuse. When something is overused or misused, then it is abused. This means to indulge in your use of TV is to waste precious time. There are people who can go to nowhere even when there is urgent need if they cannot go by personal car. This is to abuse the use of personal car. Some women will not go to the market because their car is bad. Some dare absent from meeting because their car has a breakdown(in Africa taxis are readily available and very affordable). The NIV uses the word 'engross' which means to be occupied completely or absorbed by the things one uses.

How engrossed are you in the things you own? Do they determine your devotion to God? If so then you are engrossed in them. For instance, there are some people who can absent themselves from a Sunday Fellowship Meeting because there is power failure and they are not able to press their cloths. They have been so engrossed in the use of pressing iron that their attendance to meetings depends on whether their cloths are properly pressed or not.

Some will not sing in church if the instruments are not functioning properly. They are engrossed in the use of instruments such that their ministry to God and to the brethren depends on whether the public address system and musical instruments function or not. How attached are you to the use of the things of this world? The warning is that you should not overuse or misuse them. Do not allow them to determine what you do or how you behave at any time.

> *Otherwise good things can become great obstacles to devotion and good work ethics when we become engrossed in them.*

CHAPTER THREE

THE PRESENT TIME

"And do this, understanding the present time. The hour has come for you to wake up from your slumber, because our salvation is nearer now than when we first believed. The night is nearly over; the day is almost here. So let us put aside the deeds of darkness and put on the armor of light. Let us behave decently, as in the daytime, not in orgies and drunkenness, not in sexual immorality and debauchery, not in dissension and jealousy. Rather, clothe yourselves with the Lord Jesus Christ, and do not think about how to gratify the desires of the sinful nature" (Rom 13:11-14).

"Dear children, this is the last hour; and as you have heard that the antichrist is coming, even now many antichrists have come. This is how we know it is the last hour" (I Jn 2:18).

Why must we understand the present time? It is so that we can make maximum use of it and the opportunities that come with it. If we have understood the present time then it is surely inscribed with gold ink in our hearts that "this is the last hour." If this is the last hour then we have no time left, we must make maximum use of the few minutes left. Now, if this is the last hour, the Bible prescribes what we must do.

IT IS TIME TO WAKE UP

"For it is light that makes everything visible. This is why it is said: "Wake up, O sleeper, rise from the dead, and Christ will shine on you" (Eph 5:14).

Anyone with his or her spiritual ears opened and tuned to the frequency of heaven will be conscious of the wakeup call angels in heaven have been sounding to the saints. However it seems very few people have heard and fewer still have heeded to the wake up bell. The urgency with which the bells are ringing will get everyone who is spiritually sensitive out of slumber. Anyone who is asleep is inactive and insensitive to his world. Though he may act in his dream world such actions are only illusionary. Apparently the many activities some are carrying out today are done in the dream world, for spiritually they seem to be in a very deep sleep. Is that not why we do not see the fruits of such labors, let alone the evidence that any work has been done at all? The fact that we are constantly running after the wrong things betrays our state of spiritual slumber.

WHY MUST YOU WAKE UP?

To Engage In Battle

"Wake up, wake up, Deborah! Wake up, wake up, break out in song! Arise, O Barak! Take captive your captives, O son of Abinoam"(Judges 5:12).

The average believer seems to be living under the tyranny of some sin or habit. The average believer seems to live under the tyranny of some principality or power that prevents him or her from having total freedom, and enjoying the blessing God allocates for him daily. The psalmist said, "Blessed be the Lord, who daily loadeth us with benefits, even the God of our salvation" (Ps 68:19, KJV).

Now, if we sleep all day long, how do we reap these benefits loaded into our day by the Lord? Is it not time you sound the battle song against the sins, habits and demons that seem to keep you in captivity? Is it not time to "take captive your captives"? If this must happen then the Deborah in you and the Barak in you must awake and confront reality.

Deborah means bee. The bee signifies hard work and agility. Until you wake up spiritually, the ability to work hard and be useful in nature will not be awakened. Barak means lightning. Lighting is a result of the flow of abundant charge. That which God has placed in you, to flow out to others and light up their world will not arise until you have arisen from your state of slumber. To awake here means any of the following:

Anyone with his or her spiritual ears opened and tuned to the frequency of heaven will be conscious of the wakeup call angels in heaven have been sounding to the saints.

- ❖ Open eyes
- ❖ Stir up one's self
- ❖ Lift up one's self

Hence you have to open your spiritual eyes and see what is happening around. You have to stir up yourself from complacency. Lift up yourself from that bed of indulgence.

To Behold His Face and Glory

"And I-in righteousness I will see your face; when I awake, I will be satisfied with seeing your likeness" (Ps 17:15).

"Peter and his companions were very sleepy, but when they became fully awake, they saw his glory and the two men standing with him" (Like 9:32).

If there is one need in the church of God today, it is to behold the glory of her King. But like the apostles on the mount of transfiguration many are caught in the web of spiritual slumber while the glory of the Lord is being made manifest. The truth is that until we are fully awake, let us not expect to behold the glory that brings about transformation and satisfaction. It is only when the apostles were fully awake that they saw the glory of the Lord.

Are there not many who are half awake and half-asleep? Such too cannot behold the manifestation of the glory of the King of the universe. Let us awake; adults, youths, children, ministers, "lay men and women," the mature, the maturing, the spiritual babies; so we see His face and be satisfied with beholding the glory of the Lord.

I remember, a man of God said, "You cannot look at the face of Jesus and ask for more wealth, comfort or ease." We seem to live in constant pursuit of the vain things of this world because in our slumber we have failed to see the glory of God and get hold of it. It is time to wake up and behold God's glory through His Son.

To Regain The Authentic Vision

Commenting on I King 3:16-28, in my book, "Fulfilling Your Destiny" I wrote...

"If Satan cannot completely steal what God has given a man he exchanges it with something similar but fake. Many who started with a God-given vision at some point ignorantly abandon their true pursuit for a counterfeit stuff. Why? Because at some point the vision became two; one real and one fake, and the devil took away the real thing.

In this passage, we find two ladies, the first one and her child represent the vision bearer and his vision, the second represents the devil and a counterfeit vision. We see that there was an exchange, unknown to the vision bearer. When? At midnight!

Midnight is a time when a man has stopped working and is fast asleep, a time when people are off - guard. The enemy will not come while you are watching but when you have ceased to watch.

When this evil woman took the other's living child, she did not put her dead child at some other place, but at the woman's breast. In other words there was a replacement. When Satan exchanges, he puts the false thing in the same position as the authentic and you'll continue to hold the fake as dear to you. While asleep, this woman continued to hold the fake in her very bosom. When Satan cannot steal, he exchanges what you have with something fake, in a state of spiritual slumber.

Once a man stops nursing what God gave him, Satan takes advantage of the situation and brings in something dead, and in slumber, that man may attempt to nurse the dead thing. Does that which you have appear dead? You've awaken from slumber and found that what you now hold is a dead with respect to the interests of God, dead with respect to the perishing souls of men.

Is there life in that which you're holding to?

My fear is that many vision bearers are now holding to

something dead, unknown to them. Oh that the morning may dawn for all, so that in attempting to nurse their vision they'll see it's something dead.

It takes a man real spiritual alertness to recognize that what he now holds is not alive but dead. If the woman had gotten up without attempting to nurse her baby, she would not have known that it was now dead.

That thing you're now pursuing might not be what God originally gave you. That dead thing you are holding on to is not your own!

There is need for close examination of what a man holds to see if it actually is what he should be holding. The dead baby and the living one were born about the same time. During periods of slumber things do actually change without a man knowing and he may awaken and assume that things are still the same meanwhile the difference is indeed as wide as life and death.

Have you taken time to closely examine what you are now holding to? Or do you assume that all is but normal. For how long have you been in a state of spiritual slumber? Is it not time to get up? Is it still midnight for you? Have you not seen that there has been a di - vision?"

THE NIGHT IS ALMOST OVER:

"Weeping may endure for a night but joy cometh in the morning" (Psalm 30:5 KJV).

I do not know what has caused you pain and sorrow. I do not even know how dark and intense your night has been. I do not even know for how long you have stayed in the dark. However, the good news is that the night is almost over. The pain and distress, the fright and terror, and all that comes with the night are almost over, lift up your eyes and behold the dawn. This means you should begin to shift your focus from the night towards the day.

THE DAY IS ALMOST HERE:

"So let us put aside the deeds of darkness and put on the armor of light" (Romans 13:12b).

If the night is almost over and the day is almost here, then we should get ready for action. This hour before dawn must be used in planning and preparing for what must be executed in the day. Without such planning it is certain that the day will not only take us by surprise but also, it will be wasted. So how do we prepare for the day?

Putting Aside Deeds Of Darkness

What are the deeds of darkness?
- Orgies
- Drunkenness
- Sexual Immorality
- Debauchery
- Dissension
- Jealousy

Thus, anything that has to do with sin and godlessness is a deed of darkness. All that does not conform to the teachings of the Bible is a deed of darkness and must be put aside. It is your responsibility to do it. As long as you are born again, you have been given the power to put them away.

Putting On The Armor of Light

What is this armor of light? If God is light, then, this armor of light is what is referred to as the armor of God in Ephesians 6:13. This armor is made up of:-
- ❖ Truth
- ❖ Righteousness
- ❖ Readiness to preach the gospel of peace
- ❖ Faith
- ❖ Salvation
- ❖ The Word

Every part of that armor must be in place if you are to be well prepared for the day.

> *"But you, brothers, are not in darkness so that this day should surprise you like a thief. You are all sons of the light and sons of the day. We do not belong to the night or to the darkness. So then, let us not be like others, who are asleep, but let us be alert and self-controlled. For those who sleep, sleep at night, and those who get drunk, get drunk at night. But since we belong to the day, let us be self-controlled, putting on faith and love as a breastplate, and the hope of salvation as a helmet"*(I Th 5:4-8).

If the day is almost here then it is time for you to rejoice because "joy cometh in the morning." It is not time to give up your pursuit of the truth. It is no more time to compromise the standards. It is no longer time to indulge in ease, comfort and pleasure. It is time to put on the armor of light. It is time to "behave decently as in day time." It is time to clothe yourself with the Lord Jesus Christ. It is time to shift your thoughts completely and wholly to the Lord. "Your salvation is nearer now than when you first believed" so do not give up the fight. If you have ever been part of the race, then it is now. Run as one who must win the prize, fight as one who must overcome.

CHAPTER FOUR

A TIME TO CONFRONT REALITY-1

Today's church seems to be the church in Laodicea. We appear to be red-hot for our God and his Christ but the truth is that we are lukewarm. The church today appears to be self-sufficient. It appears to be rich and have acquired wealth, needing nothing. But if we ask the Savior, the Amen, the Faithful and True witness, the Ruler of God's creation, He will reveal to us our true rating before Him. He sees us totally different from what we see ourselves.

Like the Laodicean church the Lord is saying to us "it is time for you to confront reality". The greatest problem of mankind is that man does not know that he does not know. Mankind seems to be plagued by third degree ignorance, and the church seems to be in the same web of arrogant ignorance. In the words of the Savior, our problem is that, "you do not realize that you are wretched, pitiful, poor, blind and naked" (Rev 3:17[b]).

If we are to understand the times, we must confront reality. We must admit our state of wretchedness, poverty, blindness and nakedness.

A WRETCHED CHURCH

Looking at the average believer today, will it be too much if we describe the church as wretched? Is misery and profound unhappiness not written across the faces and lives of professing Christians?

> *"Hear, O heavens! Listen, O earth! For the LORD has spoken: "I reared children and brought them up, but they have rebelled against me. The ox knows his master, the donkey his owner's manger, but Israel does not know, my people do not understand." Ah, sinful nation, a people loaded with guilt, a brood of evildoers, children given to corruption! They have forsaken the LORD; they have spurned the Holy One of Israel and turned their backs on him. Why should you be beaten anymore? Why do you persist in rebellion? Your whole head is injured, your whole heart afflicted. From the sole of your foot to the top of your head there is no soundness--only wounds and welts and open sores, not cleansed or bandaged or soothed with oil "*(Isa 1:2-6).

The plight of the church lies in her rebellion against, and negligence of, the Lord. We seem to have forsaken the Lord in pursuit of our own sectarian rules and doctrines. The word of God is maligned to sooth the doctrines of a particular group. The church seems to be plagued by wounds and welts and open sores of strife, division, disloyalty and betrayal. Are we not a people loaded with the guilt of corruption, of exposing one another to the enemy? Have we not rejoiced at the fall of a brother or ministry we considered a rival? Has today's church not turned its back on the Holy One of Israel? Have we not spurned His Name? Have we not forsaken His standards? Have we not snuffed at the commands of our God and considered them grievous, burdensome and contemptible?

It is high time, under the search light of God, each one who bears His Name examines his state and behold, through the eyes of God, his wretchedness. Is the Lord not saying to His beloved church, blood bought, spirit-birthed, ""This is what the LORD says:

> *"Your wound is incurable, your injury beyond healing. There is no one to plead your cause, no remedy for your sore, no healing for you. All your allies have forgotten you; they care nothing for you. I have struck you as an enemy would and punished you as would the cruel, because your guilt is so great and your sins so many. Why do you cry out over your wound, your pain that has no cure? Because of your great guilt and many sins I have done these things to you"* (Jer 30:12-15)?

> *If we are to understand the times, we must confront reality. We must admit our state of wretchedness, poverty, blindness and nakedness.*

There is no healing or cure of our wretchedness. Our misery has no cure but to return to the standards of God. If there is any hope for us, it lies in the embracing of the whole counsel of God. Let us not be afraid to expel the apostate brethren and assemblies, let us make clear our allegiance to the *absoluteness* of God's word, nothing subtracted.

It seems to me that the church somehow has seen her wound but rather than turning to the Lord and seeking Him, we have turned to this accursed system; to its ways, methods and values, thinking by so doing we will find healing and relief. The world is not able to bind our wound or heal our sores. We cannot find the joy that has eluded us because of our disobedience, by compromising with the values and standards of the world, embracing its hype and superficiality.

The worst aspect of our wretchedness lies not in the wounds, welts and sores but in the fact that the King is out. He is persistently knocking for us to open the door for Him to come in and heal our wounds and bring to us joy once again. But we seem to be too busy in our compromise and flirting with the world that we fail to hear His voice and open the door to Him. He wants to take away our misery and profound unhappiness and give us life, joy, peace and hope once again. And so He says, "Here I am! I stand at the door and knock. If anyone hears my voice and opens the door, I will go in and eat with him, and he with me" (Rev 3:20)!

A PITIFUL CHURCH

Today's church is one that the Lord sees as pitiful. We seem to advertise so much we cannot offer. We are far from where the Master intended for us to be. The church today is like the son of a multibillionaire who has abandoned home to live in total suffering. That which is rightfully possible for him to enjoy has been taken away because of arrogance. Like the prodigal son in Luke 15, our arrogance and quest for independence has deprived us of our power, authority, rights and privileges.

The Father, because He sees and knows all things, looks at us with much pity. We are crawling meanwhile we are meant to fly. We are attached to mediocrity meanwhile we are meant to excel. We are contented with failure meanwhile we are destined for success. We live in fear whereas we are meant to impose terror on our surroundings. We live in constant defeat meanwhile we are meant to overcome. We feed on crumbs instead of eating from the table. Why?

> *If the church returns once more to the power of the Spirit, the mountains that have stood on her way for too long a time shall be uprooted. She will begin living on the plane she was destined to.*

Because we have sold our birthright through compromise! We have abandoned the way of the Spirit: His power, counsel, leadership and direction and invented our own ways. Because we have rejected His leadership we appear as orphans. The gift of the Holy Spirit from our Lord was to provide us the covering of a Father here on earth (see John 14:18) while our Lord is away.

But because we have rejected His leading we now appear as poor miserable orphans, we live in constant oppression under the tyranny of disease, sickness, sin and fear. Our oppressors know we have rejected the Fatherhood of God through His Spirit and therefore they are exploiting our defenseless state. Shall we not submit once again and in a permanent manner to the Lordship, leadership, and loving direction of the Spirit of God? Shall we not take out of the way our rusted mechanisms of heathen methods which seem to bar the way to the Spirit?

If the church returns once more to the power of the Spirit, the mountains that have stood on her way for too long a time shall be uprooted. She will begin living on the plane she was destined to. However it has to begin with you and me. We must allow the Spirit to have His way in us and with us. Our littleness, feebleness, and weakness will disappear should we seek to be under His leadership.

A POOR CHURCH

The modern church today seems to be rich in everything but what God expects of them. We are rich in buildings, advertising methods, modernism, and technology. We seem to be rich in many things but "not rich in God-content". Where then does the poverty of the church lie?

WE ARE POOR IN POWER:

"For the kingdom of God is not a matter of talk but of power" (I Cor 4:20).

We seem to have blown our trumpet more than we can demonstrate our power and authority. There is a lot of talking, a lot of preaching, a lot of teaching, a lot of "prophesying", a lot of singing and so on and so forth, but in all these little or no power is demonstrated. The lack of miracles in many a Christian circle today is a call for concern. We have invited people time and again to "Power packed" crusades only for them to come and be witnesses to our noise making. No doubt they return unaffected by our spiritual gymnastics and refuse to come again.

Our preaching has been more of talk shows than Spirit-inspired sermons. Why is there no power? Because we are afraid to confront our compromise. Because we have failed to stand out separate. Because of the many leakages in our lives caused by careless talking, coarse joking and sin. We lack the power because we have not sought the one who gives it. We think our mechanisms can be a substitute. This is where the problem lies.

WE ARE POOR IN FAITH

"Listen, my dear brother: Has not God chosen those who are poor in the eyes of the world to be rich in faith and to inherit the kingdom He promised those who love Him" (James 2:5)?

If the word of God is true and we cannot deny its truth and infallibility, then the church is nothing but a failure. We see the exact opposite of what God intends His church to be. We see those who are rich in the eyes and things of the world, those who are rich according to the values and standards of the world but totally poor in faith. It is as if James is saying we cannot be rich by worldly standards and values and still be rich in faith. It's like the Lord is saying right now to His church, "You of little faith, why are you so afraid" (Matt 8:26[a]) or worse still He is asking us, "why are you so afraid? Do you still have no faith" (Mk 4:40)? The Lord is, I believe, shocked by the absence of faith in our lives and in the church.

We are afraid to be separate because we have no faith. We are afraid to lay all on the altar because we have no faith. We are afraid to give sacrificially because we have no faith. We are afraid to suffer for the sake of the cross because we have no faith. Our daily lives are void of miracles because we have no faith. The mountains that have stood before the church for so long a time have been there because of the lack of faith, even as small as the mustard seed. Let us acknowledge our poverty in faith, because we have refused to speak the word aloud to our spirits, because we have failed to listen with attention to the word as it is preached.

We lack faith because we have failed to memorize the word and hide it in our hearts. If we make ourselves; spirit, soul and body available to God, if we expose ourselves daily to the word of God, putting it in practice, then supernatural faith will be born in our hearts. Such faith does the impossible. It moves mountains. That is our portion by right of the redemption power given us at conversion. Let us seek to grow in faith so that we can truly inherit all that is ours in the kingdom.

> *We put our own interests before those of God and of others because we are poor in love.*

WE ARE POOR IN LOVE:

The Lord Jesus Christ made it clear, that His disciples will be recognized and identified with Him by their love for one another. "By this all men will know that you are my disciples, if you love one another" (John 13:35). Can we truly say we are disciples by the love we have shown one another? If we are unconsciously kept somewhere, say about twenty believers, and asked to live without carrying bibles, or praying in groups or proclaiming the fact that we are His disciples and observed for three days how we live and interact one with the other, will it be evident that we are lovers of one another? What will the testimony of those who will be observing us be?

Are we not poor in love? We give too little to the work of God because we are poor in the love for God. We give little to the needy around us because we are poor in love. We hoard things for ourselves because we are poor in love for fellow mankind. We preach little because we are poor in love for the sinner. We are impatient with the failure, faults and weaknesses of others because we are poor in love. We are poor in deeds of kindness and hospitality because we are poor in love. We fail to share and bear the burdens of one another because we are poor in love. There is strife and quarrelling even in circles of believers because we are poor in love. We are jealous and covet the possessions and positions of fellow brethren because we are poor in love.

We are boastful and proud of our possessions, positions and exploits because we are poor in love. We are distant, different, cold and unapproachable because we are poor in love. We put our own interests before those of God and of others because we are poor in love. We are rude because we are poor in love. We rebel against constituted authority, demand and insist on our own way because we are poor in love. We are easily angered and react to little provocations because we are poor in love.

We harbor grudges and hate because we are poor in love. We keep records of the hurts and wrongs others have caused us because we are poor in love. We are disloyal because we lack love. We expose the sins and faults of one another because we lack love. We live in constant suspicion of one another because we lack love. We do not believe one another because we lack love. We do not expect the best of others because we are poor in love. We quickly abandon and desert those in suffering because we lack love. We pray too little for one another because we are poor in love.

LET'S GET PRACTICAL

Where is the compassion you have shown the needy around you? Whose need did you meet last week? What did you sacrifice on behalf of another? Oh! That we may admit our *lovelessness*, yes our dire poverty in love, and awaken to do something about it. Let us ask the Lord to forgive us for betraying His cause. God gave and sacrificed His only Son because He loved a world that merited nothing but His righteous indignation. We too, if we must be His followers, must give ourselves and our goods even when it hurts so that others will be helped.

WE ARE POOR IN PRAISE AND WORSHIP
"Yet a time is coming and has now come when the true worshipers will worship the Father in spirit and truth, for they are the kind of worshipers the Father seeks. God is spirit, and his worshipers must worship in spirit and in truth" (John 4:23-24).

If the Father seeks true worshippers, then it means there are false worshippers. It seems the church today made up of false worshippers, those who proclaim his praise from their lips but whose hearts are far away from Him. Their lives do not conform to what they sing and declare with their lips. Have we not "worshipped" Him as King and Lord and then refused to live according to the truth of His word? Have we by our actions not sought to dethrone the One we dubiously proclaim as King? If He is King why have we refused to pay Him the tribute that rightfully belongs to Him? If He is King then why do we flirt with the one who seeks His Throne and Rule?

The Father seeks worshippers, but He seeks only those who worship Him in spirit and in truth. Where is the worship that flows from within our spirits? Have we not in many cases just memorized a few words to say during worship? The time has come when God must be worshipped in truth. There is no duplicity in truth. There is no pretense in truth. To me, God has looked at most of what we call worship and His verdict is "These people honor me with their lips, but their hearts are far from me. They worship me in vain" (Matt 15:8-9ᵃ).

We have refused to offer Him our treasures. We have "bowed down in worship and adoration" but refused to pour out the treasures in our bags. About the Magi from the east, that the Bible says, "On coming to the house they saw the child with his mother Mary and they bowed down and worshipped him. Then they opened their treasures and presented him gifts of gold and of incense and of myrrh" (Matt 2:11).

"They bowed down and worshipped him." We may be bowing down but do we really worship? If we do then where are the treasures we are presenting Him? How can we say we worship Him when all the time our treasures *For us to qualify as true worshippers of the King of the universe, we must bring our hearts in total submission to the rule of the Spirit of God.* are sealed and kept for ourselves? The result of worship is that the treasures are opened and poured out to the King. Where are our alabaster jars of very expensive perfume that we unreservedly pour out on His feet? We have often come and fallen down at His feet and even shed tears but failed to offer Him the best of our time, energy, finances, relationships, yeah the best of our lives. We are poor in praise and worship because we do not worship in spirit and in truth.

For us to qualify as true worshippers of the King of the universe, we must bring our hearts in total submission to the rule of the Spirit of God. Then our spirits will flow out to Him in truth. May all false worshippers, those who worship in the flesh and in falsehood be transformed to true worshippers so that our worship services will begin to experience the manifestations of His power and glory.

WE ARE POOR IN BLESSINGS:
"Blessed are all who fear the LORD, who walk in his ways. You will eat the fruit of your labor; blessings and prosperity will be yours. Your wife will be like a fruitful vine within your house; your sons will be like olive shoots around your table. Thus is the man blessed who fears the LORD" (Ps 128:1-4).

Why are we poor in the blessings God has put at our disposal? Because we are poor in the fear of God. We live the way we want, make the choices we want, go where we want, purchase what we want, make the friendships we want. We have refused to walk in the ways of the Lord. Where is the hatred of sin that results from the fear of the Lord? Where is the fear of compromise that results from the fear of the Lord? Why are we poor in blessings?
We are poor in blessings because we love the world.
We are poor in blessings because we live in disobedience.
We are poor in blessings because we live in sin.

We are poor in blessings because we live in daily neglect the things of God and of our relationship with Him.
We are poor in blessings because we are committed to a life of mediocrity on the plane. We have refused to climb the mountain of God – the place of excellence and experience with God.

If we are blessed, then why are the houses in such disorder? Why do we sow so much yet reap so little? If we are blessed then where is the fruitful family life? We are poor in blessings because we have failed to ascend the mountain of God and to stand in His holy presence. We are afraid of the mountain because our hands are not clean. Our hearts are not pure, and we are attached to things that have taken the place of God in our hearts, so we have failed to receive the blessings that God bestows on the mountain, His holy place (see Psalm 15:3-5).

A BLIND CHURCH:

> *"Hear, your deaf; look, you bind, and see! Who is blind but my servant, and deaf like the messenger I send? Who is blind like the one committed to me, blind like the servant of the LORD? You have seen many things, but have paid no attention; your ears are open, but you hear nothing"* (Isa 42:18-20).

We are blind because we live in total ignorance and oblivion of the signs of the times. We see things yet we fail to pay any attention to them. Where are the visions that come with spiritual sight? It seems our spiritual eyes need to be opened so that we can be able to see beyond the now. We have failed to see the coming danger because our eyes are closed. We fail to see the needs around us because we are blind. The light of God has had little effect on us because we are blind. Like Paul, many of us are wholeheartedly committed to the wrong course because scales of spiritual blindness are over our eyes.

May the Lord heal us of our blindness! May the scales fall off our eyes! May the veil be lifted up and removed from our minds. May we see our failures and turn to the Lord. May we take off the speck from our eyes so we can see clearly to be of help to a dying world! May the eyes of our hearts be enlightened that we know our calling – the hope to which we have been called; that we may know the riches of his glorious inheritance in us the saints; that we may know His incomparably great power for us who believe (see Eph 1:18-19). We have not made use of all that is ours because we have not truly seen that they are ours. O Lord, heal our blindness!

A NAKED CHURCH

"He answered 'I heard you in the garden, and I was afraid because I was naked; so I hid'" (Gen 3:10).

The Lord pointed out to the Loadicean church's nakedness, not so that, like Adam and Eve, they could run and hide but so that they could buy from Him "white clothes to wear, so that you can cover your shameful nakedness" (see Rev 3:18). The church of God seems to shy away from spiritual reality and communion because she is afraid her nakedness will be exposed. Why are we naked? Because of our self-righteousness! We have failed to clothe ourselves with Christ.

The Bible says, "Rather clothe yourselves with the Lord Jesus Christ..." (Rom 13:14[a]). Have we really clothed ourselves with Christ? Is the life of Christ seen in us and on us? Are His sorrows our sorrows, are His tears our tears? Have we really clothed ourselves with Christ? Is the life of Christ seen in us and on us? Are His interests our interests, His burdens our burdens, His sorrows our sorrows, are His tears our tears? Have we really clothed ourselves with Christ? Have we clothed ourselves with His character?

The Bible says, "Therefore, as God's chosen people, holy and dearly loved, clothe yourselves with compassion, kindness, humility, gentleness and patience...And over all these virtues put on love, which binds them all together in perfect unity" (Col 3:12, 14).

Our lack of compassion betrays our nakedness.

Our lack of kindness betrays our nakedness.
Our lack of humility betrays our nakedness.
Our lack of gentleness betrays our nakedness.
Our lack of patience betrays our nakedness.

We are naked because we are committing spiritual adultery with the world. No one can commit adultery without exposing his or her nakedness for the other partner to see. And because the church has decided to be a friend to the world, she has exposed her nakedness. "You adulterous people, don't you know that friendship with the world is hatred towards God?" (Jas 4:4[a]). By our abased standards, by our compromise, have we not adulterated ourselves with this vile world? Like the Israelites in the desert, our adultery has rendered us naked and exposed our shame before our enemy, the world. Is that not why, like Adam and Eve, we are afraid? Is that not why we are cowards who refuse to stand up for the truth? Is that not why we shy away from God's presence and spiritual reality to cover ourselves with the leaves of religion and a form of godliness which denies the very power of the latter? God help us!

CHAPTER FIVE

A TIME TO CONFRONT REALITY -2

A DEFEATED CHURCH

"The very fact that you have lawsuits among you means you have been completely defeated already. Why not rather be wronged? Why not rather be cheated? Instead, you yourselves cheat and do wrong, and you do this to your brothers" (I Cor 6:7-8).

"Jesus knew their thoughts and said to them, "Every kingdom divided against itself will be ruined, and every city or household divided against itself will not stand" (Matt 12:25).

The manifestation of our defeat lies in the fact that we are divided. The spiritual law the Lord gave in Matt 12:25 seems to have caught us. Why is there cheating and exploitation of fellow brethren? Why are there attempts to overthrow authority even in the church? Why do we find delight in hurting others?

Has the devil not succeeded to breed division in the church of God through our petty differences thereby erecting walls of hostility? We are defeated already, unless we resolve to put away our petty differences defend nothing but the Gospel and the

Kingdom. Let us put aside our own misunderstanding and misinterpretation of scripture and abide by the truth of God. Let us uphold the whole counsel of God and not portions that sooth our biased doctrine.

SEVEN MANIFESTATIONS OF DIVISION

Division is manifested through aspects. People are divided if anyone of these aspects is found amongst them. The level of the division can be measured by the level to which each of these manifestations is present. May I say that all need not be present for it to be evident that a people are divided. It suffices for one to be manifested to any degree for division to exist among any people.

The heart cry of our Lord on the night of His arrest was, "I pray also for those who will believe in Me through their message, that all of them may be one, Father, just as you are in Me and I in you." (Jn $17:20^b\text{-}21^a$). He continued, "may they be brought to complete unity to let the world know that you sent me and have loved them even as you have loved me" (Vs 23).

Thus, the oneness and unity of the church is still a burden in the heart of the risen King. It pains His heart each time He looks upon His church to behold nothing but increasing division even amongst those of the same assembly. How then can you identify the presence of division among people? Division is manifested in any of the following ways:

1.   DISCRIMINATION:

Wherever there is any form of discrimination, division reigns. If people are treated according to race, tribe, nationality, gender or any such thing, then such are operating under the spirit of division. In some Christian circles, people are treated according to their social, academic or financial status (see Jas 2:1-4). This is against the ethics of Christianity and the teaching of our Lord and Savior. We actively oppose the purpose of His death each time we build walls of division. We rebuilt what Christ came to destroy each time we sow seeds of division. The Bible says, "for He Himself is our peace, who has made the two one and has destroyed the barrier, the dividing wall of hostility" (Eph 2:14).

> *The oneness and unity of the church is still a burden in the heart of the risen King. It pains His heart each time He looks upon His church to behold nothing but increasing division.*

The walls of racism, nationalism, tribalism, classism and the like have been broken. All these walls of hostility have been destroyed, thus we work against the interest of the King and His Kingdom each time we attempt to erect them.

Now let's bring it to a personal note. How open are you in relating to people of another race, nationality, tribe, class etc. Do you relate freely with them or you are cold, reserved and distant? What about the barrier of age? Are you one who refuses to relate with the young or with the old? If so you are an enemy to the purposes of Christ.

The Bible says,
> *"You are all sons of God through faith in Christ Jesus, for all of you who were baptized into Christ have clothed yourselves with Christ. There is neither Jew nor Greek, slave nor free, male nor female, for you are all one in Christ Jesus. If you belong to Christ, then you are Abraham's seed, and heirs according to the promise"* (Gal 3:26-29).

Elsewhere it is written, "Here there is no Greek or Jew, circumcised or uncircumcised, barbarian, Scythian, slave or free, but Christ is all, and in all" (Col 3:11). That is the word of God, you must believe it and act in accordance with your belief, if not consider yourself to be bound by unbelief and you know the lot of the unbelieving (see Rev 21:8).

2.   DESPISE:

To despise means to regard as contemptible or worthless. Despise is not of God but of the devil. If you despise anybody, you are acting in line with the devil. The Bible says, "Meanwhile, the Philistine, with his shield-bearer in front of Him, kept coming closer to David. He looked David over and saw that he was only a boy, ruddy and handsome, and despised him" (I Sam 17:41-42 emphasis added).
Is there someone you regard as worthless because of his age? Is there someone you despise because of his social or financial status? Is there someone you despise because of some physical defect or illness? Despise is not of God, it is a character of the devil. Anywhere there is despise of any degree, then be sure that division reigns among the people.

Clicks in the household of God result from the fact that people take pride in some individuals to the detriment of others. They shift their focus from God to people. This was exactly the case with the Corinthian church (see I Cor 3:1-4, 4:6-7).

Is there someone whose leadership you despise? Repent of it and have your heart corrected towards that one. Is there a class of people you despise? Repent of it and have your heart corrected towards them. Is there a tribe you despise? Repent and have your heart corrected towards it. If not you are not a friend to Him who loved all and gave Himself for them. You are not obeying the scripture that says, "Do nothing out of selfish ambition or vain conceit, but in humility consider others better than yourselves" (Phil 2:3).

3. DISRESPECT:

Someone may wonder what the difference is between the previous point and this one. Well, in my opinion, despise has to do with the attitude of the mind and heart while disrespect goes beyond that, to the level of our words and actions. In many circles today, the old are not given the respect they are due and leaders are not held in the esteem and honor they deserve.

Paul wrote to Timothy saying, "The elders who direct the affairs of the church well are worthy of double honor, especially those whose work is preaching and teaching"(I Tim 5:17), but how we have thrown stones at them! How we have criticized them! How we have spoken against them and exposed them to the enemy! Do you respect those in authority, those who care and pray for you, those who teach and lead you? Do you obey them?

> *"Now Elihu had waited before speaking to Job because they were older than he. But when he saw that the three men had nothing more to say, his anger was aroused. So Elihu son of Barakel the Buzite said: "I am young in years, and you are old; that is why I was fearful, not daring to tell you what I know. I thought, `Age should speak; advanced years should teach wisdom"* (Job 32:4-7).

What is your attitude in the presence of the aged and spiritually mature? Do you struggle to speak even before you are granted permission? Are you keen to listen to their words of wisdom and insight? Elihu waited before speaking because the others were older than he. Do you sit quietly and listen when you are in the presence of spiritually more mature people? Or you think you are "Mr. know all." I am not saying that you have nothing to say but that you learn to show respect, waiting until you are given the opportunity.

To speak against those in spiritual authority with the intent to damage is to play with fire (see I Sam 26:8-9, II Sam 1:14, Eccl 10:12). So be careful before the words of your lips consume you.

Paul wrote, "… and the wife must respect her husband." (Eph 5:33) and Peter wrote, that husbands should respect their wives (I Peter 3:7). These verses together imply that the oneness that results from the marriage bond is manifested in mutual respect.

> *To speak against those in spiritual authority with the intent to damage is to play with fire*

Once that mutual respect is lacking, the bond is severed and strained. If we are to be one, if we must realize the unity that is expected of us believers, then we must respect one another. Let us kick disrespect out of our midst, for it is a manifestation of division.

4. **DISREGARD:**

Disregard talks of a lack of attention and consideration. It talks of ignoring and neglecting.

Will it be too much to say believers live in constant disregard one for another? Is that not why in one assembly many are sick, naked, hungry and homeless while others throw away food, have clothes they do not wear often, have empty rooms in their homes? If we have regard for one another how then can this form of neglect be possible?

Read the following verses and evaluate your life whether you are living in obedience to these commands.

"Carry each other's burdens, and in this way you will fulfill the law of Christ" (Gal 16:2).

"He who has been stealing must steal no longer, but must work, doing something useful with his own hands, <u>that he may have something to share with those in need</u>" (Eph 4:28, emphasis added).

"Each of you should look not only to your own interests, but also to the interests of others" (Phil 2:4).
"And do not forget to do good and to share with others, for with such sacrifices God is pleased" (Heb 13:16). In obeying these scriptures we shall develop regard for one another.

5.   **DISTRUST:**

When people live in one accord, they live in trust and loyalty to one another. Where there is disloyalty and consequently disunity people tend to doubt, distrust and suspect one another. The bond of unity is love, and when that bond is lacking disloyalty and suspicion creep in.

Do you trust your brethren? Do you trust all of them without exception? Where there is distrust and disloyalty you can be sure of strife, quarrels, envy, jealousy, malicious talking, suspicion, doubt and all kinds of friction. And where these exist, defeat is eminent.

6.   **DUPLICITY:**

Duplicity is the direct result of distrust. People tend to put on double personalities when they are not sure of their environment and the people around them. Where there is unity, there is mutual acceptance and everyone can be free to "be themselves" without fear. This lack of unity and love pushes people to become double in their personality. This usually happens with people who are not sure of themselves and want to please everybody. In a case where there are camps, people tend to put up different personalities depending on where they are or with who they are. We can see this clearly in the case of Peter in Antioch.

> *"When Peter came to Antioch, I opposed him to his face, because he was clearly in the wrong. Before certain men came from James, he used to eat with the Gentiles. But when they arrived, he began to draw back and separate himself from the Gentiles because he was afraid of those who belonged to the circumcision group. The other Jews joined him in his hypocrisy, so that by their hypocrisy even Barnabas was led astray.*
> *When I saw that they were not acting in line with the truth of the gospel, I said to Peter in front of them all, "You are a Jew, yet you live like a Gentile and not like a Jew. How is it, then, that you force Gentiles to follow Jewish customs?"*(Gal 2:11-14)

Peter, though a leader practiced duplicity, and this brought him in confrontation with Paul. In the absence of the Jews he behaved differently. He was afraid of being rejected by the Gentiles. When the Jews were present, he acted in line with them, in fear of being rejected. People with double personalities hardly stand up for the truth; rather, they often take sides with people. And because they want to get things out of people they cannot help but switch personalities in order to be at "peace".

7. DEFEAT:

There are many people in our churches today who are crushed and frustrated. The in-house fighting in many circles has left them with broken hearts and wounded consciences. In a place where there is unity everyone is victorious because victory for one means victory for all and defeat for one means defeat for all. Thus, members ensure that everyone is up and doing. But where there is division, there is the "everyone for himself" attitude and this leaves many people frustrated because when they fall there is none to lift them. James asked,

> *Seven Manifestations of division are discrimination, despise, disrespect, distrust, duplicity, disregard, and defeat. When any one of these is present, so is division.*

"What causes fights and quarrels among you? Don't they come from your desires that battle within you? You want something but don't get it. You kill and covet, but you cannot have what you want. You quarrel and fight. You do not have, because you do not ask God" (Jas 4:1-2).

Where there are quarrels and fights, there are some who have been defeated. Where there are killings, then some have been defeated.

WE MUST IDENTIFY AND CONFRONT THE ACHANS

"But the Israelites acted unfaithfully in regard to the devoted things; Achan son of Carmi, the son of Zimri, the son of Zerah, of the tribe of Judah, took some of them. So the LORD's anger burned against Israel. Now Joshua sent men from Jericho to Ai, which is near Beth Aven to the east of

Bethel, and told them, "Go up and spy out the region." So the men went up and spied out Ai.
When they returned to Joshua, they said, "Not all the people will have to go up against Ai. Send two or three thousand men to take it and do not weary all the people, for only a few men are there." So about three thousand men went up; but they were routed by the men of Ai, who killed about thirty-six of them. They chased the Israelites from the city gate as far as the stone quarries and struck them down on the slopes. At this the hearts of the people melted and became like water.

Then Joshua tore his clothes and fell facedown to the ground before the ark of the LORD, remaining there till evening. The elders of Israel did the same, and sprinkled dust on their heads. And Joshua said, "Ah, Sovereign LORD, why did you ever bring this people across the Jordan to deliver us into the hands of the Amorites to destroy us? If only we had been content to stay on the other side of the Jordan! O Lord, what can I say, now that Israel has been routed by its enemies? The Canaanites and the other people of the country will hear about this and they will surround us and wipe out our name from the earth. What then will you do for your own great name?"

The LORD said to Joshua, "Stand up! What are you doing down on your face? Israel has sinned; they have violated my covenant, which I commanded them to keep. They have taken some of the devoted things; they have stolen, they have lied, they have put them with their own possessions. That is why the Israelites cannot stand against their enemies; they turn their backs and run because they have been made liable to destruction. I will not be with you anymore unless you destroy whatever among you is devoted to destruction" (Jos 7:1-12).

There is an absolute truth in verse one with respect to today's church. Have we not acted most unfaithfully in regards to the devoted things? The Bible says, "You are not your own; you were bought at a price. Therefore honor God with your body" (see I Cor 6:19, 20). This means we are beings owned by God, set apart for His use and therefore we are devoted unto Him. If we are devoted unto the Lord then all we own is also devoted to Him. However many do live in total neglect of this truth. Many use their eyes, mouth, ears, hands and feet to serve the devil.

They look at things they should not, they utter words they should not, they listen to things they should not, they touch people and things they should not, and go to places they should not. They are acting unfaithfully in regard to their devoted body. Some wear clothes that expose their bodies and nakedness to the world; they act unfaithfully with respect to their devoted body. Some use their mind to conceive the thoughts of the devil, they have imagined evil things.

Some use their intellect to serve the cause of this world. Some steal tithes and offerings. The way we use our money shows that we are acting unfaithfully in regard to that which is devoted to God. We misuse our time and therefore rob God of what belongs to Him. We act unfaithfully with regards to our energy; we waste it on unimportant things and fail to give our all to the work of the Lord. The way some handle their children, they seem to have sold them to the world and to the devil. They are acting unfaithfully towards devoted things. The way some people behave towards their spouse shows that they are unfaithful to devoted things.

In the words of Laban to Jacob, the Lord seems to be saying to the church, "The women are my daughters, the children are my children, and the flocks are my flocks. All you see is mine" (Gen 31:43a and b).

The way some pastors act towards the flock of God makes them unfaithful towards devoted things. If we must act faithfully to the Lord in regard to all we possess then we must be willing to give Him our all. The Lord is telling us "your silver and gold are mine, and the best of your wives and children are mine" (I Kings 20:3).
If we must act faithfully, then our response must be "Just as you say, my Lord the King. I and all I have are yours." (I Kings 20:4). Will you tell Him now, that you and all you are and have is His?

Your body, relationships, business, home, car, job, money, wife, children, mind, will, emotions, intellect, intuition, communion, conscience, and yeah, all that you are and have must be made His, and His irrevocably. You must understand that you are nothing but a steward of God's property which He has entrusted to your care. You cannot afford to make the church vulnerable and defeated because of your unfaithfulness with that which is rightfully His by creation and by redemption.

Is the Lord's anger not against us because we are acting unfaithfully in regard to devoted things? Is that not why we are not able to stand against the onslaught of disease, sin and failure? Is that not why witches and other agents of darkness can sit comfortably in our midst? Is that not why we can be resisted by them right in the places we call "the house of God" or "the presence of God"? Is today's church not backing out of spiritual warfare? Are we not abandoning grounds to advancing false religions and the increasing spread of pseudo Christianity? Why do we seem to be running helter-skelter before our enemies? Why do we cower before the threat of Islam and the one world government? If we are to give an accurate description of ourselves then we would say we are a lot whose hearts have melted and become like water. We no longer have the boldness of the lion which we are supposed to have.

Are there some mourners?

"Then Joshua tore his clothes and fell face down to the ground before the ark of the LORD, remaining there till evening. The elders of elders of Israel did the same, and sprinkled just on their heads" (v 6).

Are there some in today's church who mourn the defeat of the church? Are there some who bemoan the fact that we have been fleeing from before the very enemies who are to flee before us? Are there some who have ceased from all activity and seized with sorrow because of our defeated state, are pouring out their hearts before the Throne of grace?

> *Those who consider the finances of the church as their personal finances, who have made the work of God their family affair, and use the sacrifice of others to indulge their children in luxury are the people who make the church vulnerable. They should stop and carry out restitution.*

Let us not accuse the Lord of delivering His church unto the hands of the enemy. Let us not point fingers at Him for making us powerless and vulnerable, for that will be blasphemy. We have no reason to be contented with such defeat. It is not the Lord, it is our sins, our compromise, our love of the world, yes our friendship with the world's system that has made us forfeit the power and authority which is rightfully ours. As a result, we run and hide from the enemy we have to pursue.

For those who are mourning the defeated state of the church, it is time to identify the Achans and confront them with their sins. It is true we have to pray but prayer alone will not do. The Lord is saying to the leaders who still care, "Stand up!" You must confront reality if we must regain our power and authority. We must confront the problem if we are to regain the victory.

Reasons why we cannot stand

These are the charges against the church of today:
1. The church has sinned
2. The church has violated the Lord's covenant
3. The church has taken some of the devoted things
4. The church has stolen
5. The church has lied
6. The church has put devoted things amongst their own possessions.

We have already spoken of the sin of the church, of her violation of the covenant through spiritual adultery. We have spoken of her unfaithfulness towards devoted things. We talked of her robbing God. We have spoken of her lies in worship and service. Now let us comment on the sixth point above; that of putting devoted things amongst one's own possessions. Let this sound as a warning to those ministers of the Gospel and other servants in the Lord's vineyard who do not distinguish between that which is for their personal use and that which is devoted unto God. Those who consider the finances of the church as their personal finances, who have made the work of God their family affair, and use the sacrifice of others to indulge their children in luxury are the people who make the church vulnerable. They should stop and carry out restitution.

> It is written that,
> "Joy is gone from our hearts; our dancing has turned to mourning. The crown has fallen from our head. Woe to us, for we have sinned! Because of this our hearts are faint, because of these things our eyes grow dim" (Lam 5:15-17).

Why are we defeated? Because we have sinned and so "Joy is gone from our hearts". How then can we stand against the enemy when we have no strength? If joy is gone we are left with nothing but to grieve. And one who grieves has no strength to stand in battle. Nehemiah understood this and therefore said to the Jews, "Go and enjoy choice food and sweet drinks, and send some to those who have nothing prepared. This day is sacred to our Lord. Do not grieve, for the joy of the Lord is your strength." (Neh 8:10). Now if this joy of the Lord that is supposed to be our strength has departed from our hearts, how can we face the enemy? How can we stand when our hearts are faint? The effects of the charges against us are that:

1. The church cannot stand against her enemies
2. She turns her back and runs because she has been made liable to destruction
3. The Lord's presence is no longer with her.

The Solution

Now we have presented the problem, what then is the solution? The answer lies in verse 13.

1. Consecration
2. Removing what is "devoted" from among us.

First we must sanctify ourselves by purifying our hearts. We must dedicate our lives entirely to Him. That is the beginning of the solution. Secondly we must purge from our homes and our midst all that rightfully belongs to God and His people. All we needed to have given to the work of the Lord and to the needy around us, but which we have kept for ourselves must be removed. Thirdly, we must find out who the Achans are amongst us (those living in active and deliberate sin) and purge the church of them. Unless these things are done, we shall remain vulnerable.

In verse 13, the people had to be consecrated as a group and also as individuals. Thus you must play your role, and as each one plays his role in the consecration process, the leader should consecrate the people of God. Let us not fail to confront the Achans and expel them from among God's people.

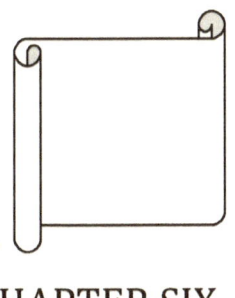

CHAPTER SIX

A TIME TO CONFRONT REALITY-3

A LEPROUS CHURCH

"Then Naaman and all his attendants went back to the man of God. He stood before him and said, "Now I know that there is no God in all the world except in Israel. Please accept now a gift from your servant."

The prophet answered, "As surely as the LORD lives, whom I serve, I will not accept a thing." And even though Naaman urged him, he refused...After Naaman had traveled some distance, Gehazi, the servant of Elisha the man of God, said to himself, "My master was too easy on Naaman, this Aramean, by not accepting from him what he brought. As surely as the LORD lives, I will run after him and get something from him."

So Gehazi hurried after Naaman. When Naaman saw him running toward him, he got down from the chariot to meet him. "Is everything all right?" he asked.

"Everything is all right," Gehazi answered. "My master sent me to say, `Two young men from the company of the prophets have just come to me from the hill country of Ephraim. Please give them a talent of silver and two sets of clothing.'"

"By all means, take two talents," said Naaman. He urged Gehazi to accept them, and then tied up the two talents of silver in two bags, with two sets of clothing. He gave them to two of his servants, and they carried them ahead of Gehazi. When Gehazi came to the hill, he took the things from the servants and put them away in the house. He sent the men away and they left. Then he went in and stood before his master Elisha.
"Where have you been, Gehazi?" Elisha asked.
"Your servant didn't go anywhere," Gehazi answered.

But Elisha said to him, "Was not my spirit with you when the man got down from his chariot to meet you? Is this the time to take money, or to accept clothes, olive groves, vineyards, flocks, herds, or menservants and maidservants? Naaman's leprosy will cling to you and to your descendants forever." Then Gehazi went from Elisha's presence and he was leprous, as white as snow" (I Kings 5:15-16, 19-27).

Some brethren have understood that for us to stand separate from the world, we must refuse its offers under any and every circumstance. They have understood that we cannot accept what the world offers without accepting the sins and woes of the world. The compromise and mediocre standards of holiness and consecration existing in church today stem from the simple fact that many in the service of the King have run after that which the King has rejected by His death on the cross. The diseases of the world are creeping fast into the church of God because His servants are running after the offers of God's enemy. In doing this a lot of compromise comes into play: falsehood, duplicity, hypocrisy, blatant lies telling, fraud etc. are practiced.

How many have compromised the truth before today's "Naamans" in order to get their offer. They run after the money of those who refuse to bow completely and totally to the cross. Such men "serve the Lord" but also bow down before the god of Mammon and this world. They have pretended to receive gifts for the sake of God's people, the poor, and the Gospel but the bitter truth is that they receive it for personal use. They have it stored in personal accounts and in monumental buildings they have erected for themselves.

We cannot run after the offers of this world and come before the King like those who are not guilty. If we open our ears we shall hear the Lord asking us, "where have you been?" Unlike Gehazi we should be honest to say, "…running after the world in compromise" and not pretend to say, "Your servant didn't go anywhere". To Gehazi, running after Naaman and standing in Elisha's presence was the same thing. He saw no difference between them. There are many in the service of the King who do not see any difference between running after the world and serving the King. To them it is one and the same thing.

They see no difference between flirting with the world and consecration unto God. Their faith is to run after the gold and clothing the Naamans can offer, and the offer always seems to be more than what they demand. The question God is asking His children in general and ministers in particular is this: "Is this time to take money, or to accept clothes, olive groves, vineyards, flocks, herds, or menservants and maidservants?" Can you give an answer to that question? There is a mad rush today for money, and a mad rush not only for clothes but for fashion and property. If we have understood that the time is short, then we have to give away the little we have so that this Gospel spreads to the furthermost parts of planet earth. The sad thing is that because of our compromise with the world and her Naamans we have made the church vulnerable to their leprosy.

> *If we are not careful, our sin and compromise will sap away our saltiness and render us unfit for the task of preserving the earth and giving it the taste it deserves.*

The sins of the world are creeping even into the church; Bigamy, lesbianism, homosexuality, pedophilia, adultery, fornication and incest are committed even among those who dare to His Name. That is why the diseases and curses associated with these sins are found even in the church today. Let this warning ring out to the Gehazis, the Lord will not sit quiet forever and watch them make His church vulnerable. In less than no time He will bring them to account.

HAVE WE LOST OUR SALTINESS?

Speaking to His disciples the Lord Jesus said, "You are the light of the world" (Matt 5:14[a]) and indeed that is what we are, the light of the world. However it seems to me that we have shone our light on the wrong path for the world to follow. We have failed to show the world the way of the cross by our life style and values. Our daily choices seem to show them the opposite of the cross. We remain the light of this world, just that we are shinning on the wrong paths. Worse still, it seems our light has been enveloped in compromise, worldly standards, values and methods.

My concern lies in the fact that we seem to have lost our saltiness. Are we indeed the salt of the earth? Is the earth truly benefiting from our presence? Then why is moral decadence permanently on the rise? Well, may be because we have not allowed the earth to have a full dose of our saltiness because of ease and self-sparing.

> *"You are the salt of the earth. But if the salt loses its saltiness, how can it be made salty again? It is no longer good for anything, except to be thrown out and trampled by men"* (Matt 5:13).

If the Lord warned that salt could lose its saltiness, it means if we are not careful, our sin and compromise will sap away our saltiness and render us unfit for the task of preserving the earth and giving it the taste it deserves. Again I ask: have we lost our saltiness? If so then we must be ready to be thrown out and trampled by men.

The way the church is treated today, it is as if men are already trampling on her. She is no longer held in esteem and respect because of the sins of her leaders. If men are already trampling on the church, then we have been thrown out because we have lost our saltiness. May God help us to preserve and maintain the saltiness that still remains! May those who have theirs intact allow nothing to leak away!

CHAPTER SEVEN

A TIME TO REBUILD THE FOUNDATIONS

Let me begin this chapter by defining the key words of its title.

A foundation, as defined by the international edition of the Funk and Wagnals dictionary is "That by which anything is founded and by which it is supported or sustained."

Looking at this definition in relation to scripture, a foundation can be considered:

1. <u>a physical structure:</u>
   ""Suppose one of you wants to build a tower. Will he not first sit down and estimate the cost to see if he has enough money to complete it? For if he lays the foundation and is not able to finish it, everyone who sees it will ridicule him"(Luke 14:28-29).

   Every building has a foundation, and this foundation is a physical structure that holds and keeps the building in place.

2. <u>Principles and Values:</u>

> *"In love a throne will be established; in faithfulness a man will sit on it-- one from the house of David-- one who in judging seeks justice and speeds the cause of righteousness"(Is 16:5).*

> *"Righteousness and justice are the foundation of your throne; love and faithfulness go before you"(Ps 89:14).*

> *"if I am delayed, you will know how people ought to conduct themselves in God's household, which is the church of the living God, the pillar and foundation of the truth"(I Ti 3:15).*

From these passages we see that a foundation can be a set of principles and values on which something is built, supported or sustained, without such values there is no support or sustenance and so everything crumbles.

What are some of these principles and values as seen in the passages above?
- Love
- Faithfulness
- Justice
- Truth
- righteousness

These are the values by which God established His throne.

3. People

"Consequently, you are no longer foreigners and aliens, but fellow citizens with God's people and members of God's household, built on the foundation of the apostles and prophets,

with Christ Jesus himself as the chief cornerstone" (Eph 2:19-20).

The bible talks of the apostles and the prophets as being the foundation of the Christian life. Thus people can also be the foundation of something. These are usually those who were at the very beginning of the existence of any society or organization. They are the ones who sustain the organization or society either by their presence or by laid down principles. They know the values and principles by which the society was built. You cannot keep them or their opinions aside and then expect things to continue to hold together. Sidelining them is pulling out part of the foundation. That is why we hear of founding fathers.

Paul wrote,
"For God, who was at work in the ministry of Peter as an apostle to the Jews, was also at work in my ministry as an apostle to the Gentiles. James, Peter and John, <u>those reputed to be pillars</u>, gave me and Barnabas the right hand of fellowship when they recognized the grace given to me. They agreed that we should go to the Gentiles, and they to the Jews"(Gal 2:8-9, emphasis added).

Paul knew that in spite of his anointing and calling he could not sideline the apostles, who were the pillars and then succeed in his ministry. There are spiritual principles which no one can violate.
The Lord said, "Him who overcomes I will make a pillar in the temple of my God" (Rev 3:12a).
Pillars are the visible part of the foundation of any great structure. That is why Samson, when he wanted to destroy the Philistines went for the pillars of their city hall.

A DIVINE PRINCIPLE

The psalmist said, "In the beginning you laid the foundations of the earth, and the heavens are the works of Your hands" (Ps 102:25).

The Almighty, Omniscient, Omnipotent God understood that, this earth could not be established if it has no foundations. That is why "in the beginning..." the first thing He did was to establish the foundations of the earth. The word here is in plural meaning there are many foundations. He established a physical structure, He established precepts, principles and values on which His earth is founded and supported.

God in His wisdom knew that for this earth to continue to exist there must be laws and values which govern it. So it was the first thing He did. Now the Bible says, "in the beginning God..." (Genesis 1:1) and elsewhere, "in the beginning was the Word..." (John 1:1).

A Combination of these two verses with Ps 102:25 shows that God and His word are the foundations of this earth. If you take God out of this earth, everything crumbles, for He forms an integral part of all that exists in the universe. If you take the word of God out of this earth everything will fall apart. Just as a foundation holds the entire building together, so does the Son of God-the word incarnate hold all things together. "He is before all things, and in Him all things hold together" (Col 1:17).

The second keyword of this chapter is "to rebuild", which means to build again. This implies that what is to be built existed already. The reason for rebuilding anything is either because the existing one was problematic, probably because the wrong material was used; or it is in poor irreparable condition and thus the only option is to rebuild.

Having defined those terms, we have established the premise for all we will say in this chapter. By the end of this chapter you should have answered three questions:

1. Do you have a foundation?
2. What is your foundation made of?
3. What is the state of your foundation?

I strongly believe this is the time to rebuild the foundations at all levels and unless we answer these questions squarely and honestly we shall see no need for the urgent rebuilding.

DO YOU HAVE A FOUNDATION?

The foundation of the Christian life is repentance: true, radical, and total repentance. Unless you repented of your sins, forsook and abandoned them, you have no foundation. Your Christian life has been like a balloon in the air, blown and tossed by the wind. In Hebrew 6:1 the Bible talks of the foundation of repentance.

It seems, many are trying to build spiritual monuments without this foundation of repentance. That is why many lives are nothing but wrecks, because the high and mighty foundationless towers are crumbling on them. Because repentance is the foundation of the Christian life, John the Baptist began his ministry by preaching, "Repent, for the kingdom of God is near" (Matt 3:2).

The Lord Jesus Christ began His ministry by calling people to repentance. He said, "The kingdom of God is near. Repent and believe the good news" (Mk 1:15). Without repentance, you have not begun the Christian life and therefore you have no foundation. Did you forsake and abandon all you knew as sin at the beginning of your Christian life or you just joint an assembly of people? Maybe you just wanted a place to practice your religion, a place to belong to so that in case of calamity you are not left alone.

Such people without this foundation see the church as some social club to belong to. Are many assemblies not proselytizing instead of making disciples? They get people into clubs because the message of the cross is never preached and repentance is far from carried out. Such assemblies of people have no foundation. It is time they pull down these "structures" and begin by building the foundation of repentance.

They have never had a foundation, so we cannot talk of rebuilding. They have to be built by preaching the message of the cross and bringing the people in contact with the life-transforming message of the cross from where true, radical and total repentance flows forth.

> *The foundation of the Christian life is repentance: true, radical, and total repentance. Unless you repented of your sins, forsook and abandoned them, you have no foundation.*

WHAT IS YOUR FOUNDATION MADE OF?

For those whose answer to the first question was in the affirmative, the second question you must face is that of the material your foundation is made of. The foundation is right or wrong depending on its depth, but primarily on the quality of the material used in its construction. "See, I lay a stone in Zion, a tested stone, a precious cornerstone for a sure foundation; the one who trusts will never be dismayed" (Isa 28:16).

"For no one can lay any Foundation other than the one already laid, which is Jesus Christ" (I Cor 3:11).

Are our churches not made up of people who have never come in contact with the Christ? They have never have a life-transforming encounter with the one who changes lives, they have not fallen on the stone and are not broken to pieces. Let me ask you a personal question: Did you come to Christ because you saw yourself a wretched sinner on his way to hell, who could do nothing to save himself, and so decided to come to the One who alone saves from sin?

Were you desperate and tired of your life of sin and so responded to the invitation of the one who alone uplifts the crushing burdens of sin? If not then your foundation is faulty. If you came to Christ because you wanted healing then your foundation is faulty. If you came to Christ because you wanted deliverance, then your foundation is faulty. If you came to Christ because you wanted provision of your needs, then your foundation is faulty. If you came to Christ because you wanted protection, then your foundation is faulty.

The Son of God was revealed to us and sent primarily as the Savior. All the other benefits are the byproducts of salvation, for a man can receive them and still go to hell if he does not come to Jesus to be saved from sin. The one who experiences a life transforming encounter with Christ does things for the sole sake of Christ.

Let me ask you another question: what motivates you in life, what determines your actions and choices? Are they based on the example of Christ? Are they based on His honor, the reputation of His Name? Are they based on his glory and approval? Have you had an encounter with the King? If not, your foundation is faulty, it must be rebuilt.

Is your life modeled according to the Word of God? Are your actions founded on the word of God? Are your words founded on the word of God? Are the principles, standards and values governing your life in accordance with God's revealed Word? If not, your foundation is faulty. Jesus said,

> *"Therefore everyone who hears these words of mine and puts them into practice is like a wise man who built his house on the rock. The rain came down, the streams rose, and the winds blew and beat against that house; yet it did not fall, because it had its foundation on the rock. But everyone who hears these words of mine and does not put them into practice is like a foolish man who built his house on sand. The rain came down, the streams rose, and the winds blew and beat against that house, and it fell with a great crash"* (Matt 7:24-27).

The word of God is the foundation of all the actions of the believer. And unless one's actions are based on the word of God, one cannot stand the test of time. It does not suffice to listen to the word of God being taught. We must get to the level of practicing it. Only such practice can lay a solid foundation.

In scripture, the rain, the stream and the wind are always representative of the spirit of God. We are expecting an outpouring of the Holy Spirit, we are desperately praying for revival. When revival comes will it be to your blessing or to your destruction? God will surely pour out His Spirit upon His church in mighty torrents which shall beat against every human house. Lives that are founded and modeled according to the Word of God will stand but those that are not will fall with a great crash. I believe the delay of this outpouring is because God is giving us time to rebuild our faulty foundations so that the revival will bring us nothing but His blessings.

Is your foundation made of rock or sand, of the word of God or your personal choices? Let us learn from nature. When rain falls in torrents, some plants are pulled down, and so the rain that was to be a blessing rather destroys them. Others who are deeply rooted on solid ground benefit from the freshness brought by the rain. It shall be the same with us, when the rain of God falls upon His church. All that is shallow and standing on a faulty ground will be pulled down but all that is deeply rooted will survive.

Is the solid foundation of holiness in your life? Is your life set apart for God? Are you living a sanctified and consecrated life? For holiness is God's solid foundation and unless your life stands on this foundation of holiness, your foundation is the wrong kind.

"Nevertheless, God's solid foundation stands firm, sealed with this inscription: 'The Lord knows those who are his', and 'Everyone who confesses the name of the Lord must turn away from wickedness'" (2 Tim 2:19) unless you are committed to live holy at all cost, the foundation of your Christian life and work remains faulty. It must be pulled down and rebuilt.

Whether you like it or not, one thing is sure; God is committed to destroy all that is built on the wrong foundation, whether they be ministries, homes, relationships, businesses, vocations etc. It is time to examine your foundations and see if they are right. Examine all including the people who matter in your life and ministry, that is, those who support or sustain you, the principles, standards and values that govern your life and ministry.

"'Therefore this is what the Sovereign LORD says: In my wrath I will unleash a violent wind, and in my anger hailstones and torrents of rain will fall with destructive fury.

> *I will tear down the wall you have covered with whitewash and will level it to the ground so that its foundation will be laid bare. When it falls, you will be destroyed in it; and you will know that I am the LORD. So I will spend my wrath against the wall and against those who covered it with whitewash. I will say to you, "The wall is gone and so are those who whitewashed it, those prophets of Israel who prophesied to Jerusalem and saw visions of peace for her when there was no peace, declares the Sovereign LORD"*(Ezekiel 13:13-16).

God will not destroy the wall and spare its builders. Both will be destroyed. He will expose all that is faulty, built on the wrong foundation. No matter how it has been painted or decorated to appear solid and strong, the violent wind of God and the coming torrents of rain will crumble all such counterfeit works. How it appears on the outside or how gorgeously successful it has been does not matter. The height to which it has risen is also not important. All that matters God is whether the foundation is made of the right material or not.

Does your outward appearance reflect what God sees inside of you? Are you just a hollow and rotten whitewashed wall? Are you covering your sin with activities? Are you covering your greed and lust for materialism with so-called faith messages? The primary work of faith is to bring about a full salvation experience. How can your own faith fail to save you from sin and bondage to self and only bring you material blessings? Can you not see the deception in which you have lived?

I am not saying that faith does not bring material or financial prosperity but that these are only secondary works of faith. Let us see how your faith has set you free from sin and self, let us see how faith has enabled you to put on the character of Christ and we will believe that it brought you financial and material prosperity. It is time you begin tearing down those whitewashed walls of yours before God does it.

You have been warned. Let the wise and simple in heart understand and obey. Let those prophets who are seeing visions of peace and prosperity; those prophets preaching messages of ease and comfort in a time when we should all be engaged in a full scale war be careful. It is time to call the people out on a full scale war against the forces of darkness. It is time to exhort the people to live as those in a battle front. It is time to exhort them to live sacrificially and give all for the Gospel's course. It is time to rebuild the foundations.

> *The primary work of faith is to bring about a full salvation experience.*

Now those who have a foundation made up of the right material in light of the Spirit of God and of the scriptures examined above will have to answer a third question: What is the state of your foundation? You say you have a foundation, and that the foundation is made of the right substance, true, but what about the state of the foundation? Is it still intact? Can you honestly and wholeheartedly say your foundation is still in order? Well as we handle this third question, you will be able to tell if the foundation of your life, the foundation of your ministry, and the foundation of the church are still in a good state.

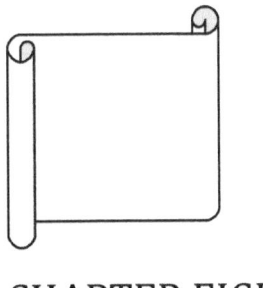

CHAPTER EIGHT

A TIME TO RUBUILD THE FOUNDATIONS-2

WHAT IS THE STATE (CONDITION) OF YOUR FOUNDATION?

What principles, values and standards, in accordance with the word of God, did you establish at the beginning of your Christian life? Are those principles still there? Are those values still held to? Are those standards still kept? Is it evident to you and more so to those around you that you still live by them? If not, then your foundation has been tampered with. It is not in the right condition.

Are the values of truth and integrity still part of your life? Are the standards of purity and separation unto God still part of your life? Are the principles of "Jesus first" and "All for God" still evident in your life and work? If not, your foundation is in a poor state.

Who mattered at the beginning of your spiritual life and work? Are those people still involved? Are you still accountable to them? Have you sidelined those who can correct and rebuke you and drawn close to those whose only response is "do as you please, the Lord is with you"? Have you driven away the Micaiahs and gathered all the Zedekiahs?

Who are the mature people in the faith who still guide and direct your path? Has your pride and arrogance driven you away from them? Let me ask you once again: are those who mattered at the beginning still involved? If not, then the bitter truth is that like Rehoboam you are in for a great fall. The work of God in your hands will crumble because the foundation is no longer solid. Your personal life is also at stake because you have pulled out the pillars that acted as a support. What about the principles, values and standards on which your ministry was founded? Were they in accordance with God's word? If so are they still followed and upheld?

> *Many of us live carelessly; we do not daily watch our values and standards, whether they are improving of falling. We seem only to be caught up with activities and the apparent results they bring.*

The sad truth is that, many of us live carelessly; we do not daily watch our values and standards, whether they are improving of falling. We seem only to be caught up with activities and the apparent results they bring. Moses told the Israelites "only <u>be careful</u>, and <u>watch</u> yourselves closely so that you do not forget the things your eyes have seen or let them slip from your heart as long as your live" (Deut 4:9^a). Keeping one's foundation in the right condition can only be done through care and watchfulness:

- ❖ Being careful about what you think
- ❖ Being careful about what you say

- ❖ Being careful about what you do
- ❖ Being careful about your inclinations
- ❖ Being watchful over your spiritual standards
- ❖ Being watchful over your propensities.

These will let you know if your standards are improving or falling. You should be able to know if you are going deeper or superficial. Being careful and watchful over oneself is the secret to spiritual aliveness. You must watch yourself closely to see that you are not abandoning your spiritual values. There are some who watch others but fail totally to watch themselves.

For a watchman to watch effectively he must watch himself closely that he is not overtaken by sleep. Peter stepped onto the water, by faith, at the invitation of Jesus, and after walking on the water for some time, the Bible says; "But when he saw the wind, he was afraid and, <u>beginning to sink</u>, cried out, "Lord save me!" (Matt 14:30, emphasis mine). Peter sounded the alarm at the very beginning. Had he not been watchful of himself he could not have noticed when he started sinking. His watchfulness caused him to cry out for help immediately he started sinking.

Your primary responsibility is to watch yourself closely. You must raise the alarm for help immediately things start going wrong with your foundation. You must not wait until your whole life has sunk into the mire. You may cry for help then, but it will be difficult for anyone to hear you from beneath the mire. You must watch and guard against your weaknesses. You must watch to see if your environment is having a negative bearing on you or vice versa. You must watch closely to ensure that your heart does not loose grip of spiritual truths.

Guard your heart

Revelations and illuminations are spiritual treasures which determine the state of a man's foundation, they must be jealously guarded. The secret to keep your foundation in tact is to watch your heart, and ensure that it keeps the truths it already knows and avoid what is not helpful.

"My son, pay attention to what I say; listen closely to my words. Do not let them out of your sight, keep them within your heart; for they are life to those who find them and health to a man's whole body. Above all else, guard your heart, for it is the wellspring of life. Put away perversity from your mouth; keep corrupt talk far from your lips. Let your eyes look straight ahead, fix your gaze directly before you. Make level paths for your feet and take only ways that are firm. Do not swerve to the right or the left; keep your foot from evil" (Prov. 4:20-27).

How do you guard your heart?
- ❖ Pay attention to God's word   verse 20
- ❖ Read God's word   verse 21
- ❖ Watch what you say   verse 24
- ❖ Watch what you see   verse 25
- ❖ Watch where you go   verse 26
- ❖ Stay focused   verse 27

Verse 23 says, "Above all else ..." The greatest service you can offer yourself, those you serve or lead, and the Kingdom of God is to guard your heart. Watch your desires and watch your beliefs.

Deuteronomy 4:15-16 continue to emphasize the need to watch oneself.
"Therefore watch yourselves very carefully, so that you do not become corrupt ..."

My brother you must watch yourself not to become corrupted for fame, power and money. You must watch your beliefs and ideas that they do not become corrupt. You must watch yourself against corrupt desires. You must watch against idolatry of any form. Do not allow yourself to be made the idol of people. You must watch yourself against returning to old bad habits and sins. You must watch yourself so as not to become enslaved by your passions. You must watch yourself so as not to become like the people around you through sinful compromise.

> *You must watch yourself not to become corrupted for fame, power and money*

You must be careful about your relationships!
You must be careful about your choices!
You must be careful about your priorities!
You must be careful about your commitments!
You must be careful about the promises you make. Be careful the way you spend time. Be careful the way you spend your energy. Be careful the way you spend your finances and other resources. By these you will be able to know the state of your foundation.
"Keep a close watch on all you do and think" (I Ti 4:16, TLB).

THE HARD REALITY

Activism is futile when the foundations are in a deplorable state. Things cannot hold together on a broken foundation. Unless we rebuild the foundations, all we do will just be a waste of time. The psalmist asked in desperation, "When the foundations are being destroyed, what can the righteous do" (Ps 11:3)?
"If the foundations be destroyed, what can the righteous do?" (Ps 11:3, KJV).

One thing is sure, when the foundations are not in a good condition there is nothing the righteous can do.

When the foundations are being destroyed, what can the activities of the righteous do?

When the foundations are being destroyed, what can the prayers of the righteous do?
When the foundations are being destroyed, what can the fasts of the righteous do?
When the foundations are being destroyed, what can the preaching of the righteous do?
When the foundations are being destroyed, what can the teachings of the righteous do?
When the foundations are being destroyed, what can the prophecies of the righteous do?
When the foundations are being destroyed, what can the praises of the righteous do?

Have you seen the need to know the state of your foundation before continuing your work? There can be no lasting results unless the foundations are rebuilt. The devil understands this, and so he will rather have us continue with our conferences, prayers, fasts, praises, preaching, teaching, giving, and prophesying than allow us confront the broken state of our foundations and do something about it. He will rather have us raise altars in a state of broken foundations because he knows they have little effect, if any. Let us not take sides with him, rather let us get to the business of rebuilding the foundations.

Foundations first!

"On the first day of the seventh month they began to offer burnt offerings to the LORD, though the foundation of the LORD's temple had not yet been laid"(Ezra 3:6).

When the Israelites returned from exile, they went straight to their usual activities, built an altar without having laid the foundation of the temple, which was their pride and symbol of God's presence among them. They failed to lay the foundations and so their enemies were not disturbed by all they did as long as there were no foundations. Their praises, prayers and sacrifices brought little or no results. Their enemies watched and even mocked at them. Are the enemies (false religions, the world, the devil and his hosts) of God's church not mocking at it? Have they not taken note that our foundations are broken and therefore nothing we do will be of lasting impact? Why do we lack joy, Spirit inspired joy? Because the foundations are in shambles!

"When the builders laid the foundation of the temple of the LORD, the priests in their vestments and with trumpets, and the Levites (the sons of Asaph) with cymbals, took their places to praise the LORD, as prescribed by David king of Israel. [11] With praise and thanksgiving they sang to the LORD: "He is good; his love to Israel endures forever. "And all the people gave a great shout of praise to the LORD, because the foundation of the house of the LORD was laid"(Ezra 3:10-11).

When the people set out to rebuild foundations of the temple, their enemies were set to panic. Until now they were unmoved because they understood all what the people did would amount to nothing as long as the foundation of the temple was not laid. As soon as the foundation was laid,

> *"Then the peoples around them set out to discourage the people of Judah and make them afraid to go on building. They hired counselors to work against them and frustrate their plans during the entire reign of Cyrus king of Persia and down to the reign of Darius king of Persia... The king should know that the Jews who came up to us from you have gone to Jerusalem and are rebuilding that rebellious and wicked city. They are restoring the walls and repairing the foundations"* (Ezra 4:4-5, 12).

The enemy understands that when the people of God begin rebuilding their foundations, his whole realm is in trouble. He knows that with our foundations in order, our prayers, fasts, praises, preaching, and teachings, will cause the greatest havoc to his kingdom in the shortest time. He will rather spend all he has than have the people of God rebuild their foundations. He understands he will no longer have access to the finances, health, and property of God's people. He knows the loss his kingdom is going to suffer. He knows the disgrace that will be done to him and so he seeks to prevent us from rebuilding our foundations.

O God, cause Your people to take sides with You and get to rebuild their personal foundations, the foundations of their work and ministries. Let the leaders of Your people take them back to the founding principles of Your Church.

WHERE TO START

Where do we start this process of rebuilding the foundations? For effectiveness we should begin rebuilding the foundations of our personal lives. It must start with us rebuilding our individual spiritual foundations. Examine the motive and reasons for which you believed. If they are wrong, correct them by dedicating yourself wholly to God because He is God and not for what you can get out of your relationship with Him. Allow the word of God to become the standard and basis of your choices, actions, relationships, values, investments, taste etc. Commit yourself to obey the word at all cost.

Next, we must build the home which is the foundation of society and an integral part of the church. As long as the homes are in disarray the church and the society cannot stand. Let husbands and wives get to mend their broken relationships. Let ministers abandon preaching until they have set their homes in order. Let unity be established in the home if it must be established in the church. Let spouses forgive and restore each other to their hearts and get to pray, once again, one with the other.

Let the husbands take their responsibility of meeting the needs of their wives and children. Let the men take up the priestly responsibility over their homes. Let integrity be restored in the homes. Let believers make their homes the place of devotion to God that they ought to be. Let parents and children get along with each other. Let the homes become, once again, sanctuaries and not the film halls and night clubs and bars they have become today.

After rebuilding the foundation of the home, the church must return to the cross. She must return to the creeds of the faith laid down by the apostles and founding fathers of Christianity. Let us not cause them pain as they watch us derail from the truths they laid down their lives for. Let us return to the standards of holiness, self-sacrifice and love they laid down for us. That is where we must begin.

WHAT HAPPENS WHEN THE FOUNDATIONS ARE REBUILT?

1. The enemy is set to panic and confusion
   (see Ezra 4:12-18)
   When you rebuild your foundations, the enemies of your life, home, and ministry will be set to panic. Sickness, sin, and demons will be set into confusion. If the church rebuilds her foundations, false religions, the world, and Satan will be set to panic and confusion. An enemy set into panic and confusion is on the verge of defeat.

2. Joy is restored:
   (see Ezra 3:10-11)
   When you rebuild your foundation the joy of the Lord will fill your heart and life. It will flood your ministry and home. When the church rebuilds her foundation, the joy of the Lord will be her strength.

3. Blessings flow in abundance:
   "'From this day on, from this twenty-fourth day of the ninth month, give careful thought to the day when the foundation of the LORD's temple was laid. Give careful thought: Is there yet any seed left in the barn? Until now, the vine and the fig tree, the pomegranate and the olive tree have not borne fruit." 'From this day on I will bless you'" (Hag 2:18-19).

   The blessings of God will fill every area of your life as you rebuild your foundations. His financial blessings, blessings of good health, material and spiritual blessings will fill your whole life. If you will rebuild the foundations of your home, then God will not only bless your home but will make it a blessing to all who come there. Your wife and children will be blessed. Strangers who come to your home will be blessed.

> *"This is what the LORD Almighty says: "You who now hear these words spoken by the prophets who were there when the foundation was laid for the house of the LORD Almighty, let your hands be strong so that the temple may be built. Before that time there were no wages for man or beast. No one could go about his business safely because of his enemy, for I had turned every man against his neighbor. But now I will not deal with the remnant of this people as I did in the past," declares the LORD Almighty. "The seed will grow well, the vine will yield its fruit, the ground will produce its crops, and the heavens will drop their dew. I will give all these things as an inheritance to the remnant of this people"*
> (Zechariah 8:9-12).

4. <u>You will know safety</u>:
   A lot of believers live in insecurity. When the foundations are rebuilt, God says you will live in safety and confidence.

5. <u>You will know peace</u>:
   The Lord will grant you peace with your enemies, in fact because of the panic and confusion they will come and seek peace with you.

   > *When the foundations are rebuilt, you enter into a new dimension of blessings, abundant joy, victory over your enemies, peace and safety.*

CHAPTER NINE

OUR RESPONSE

With all that has been said so far, the Spirit of God seems to be making one call, "it is time to seek the Lord" (see Hos 10:12). If we have ever heard this call, it has never been with such urgency. Like the prophet Hosea, I feel like shouting it out, "come, let us return to the Lord" (Hos 6:1a). Let us draw near to God so that He may draw near to us. Let us return to intimacy, let us return to Bible standards, let us return to the power of the Holy Spirit.

A TIME TO SEEK THE LORD

> *"Sow for yourselves righteousness, reap the fruit of unfailing love, and break up your unplowed ground; for it is time to seek the LORD, until he comes and showers righteousness on you"* (Hos 10:12).

> *"Seek the LORD while he may be found; call on him while he is near. Let the wicked forsake his way and the evil man his thoughts. Let him turn to the LORD, and he will have mercy on him, and to our God, for he will freely pardon"* (Isa 55:6-7).

"All night long on my bed I looked for the one my heart loves; I looked for him but did not find him. I will get up now and go about the city, through its streets and squares; I will search for the one my heart loves" (Song of Songs 3:1-2a).

It is time for us as individuals to begin to seek the Lord in a new and fresh way. It is time, to sow the seed of righteousness everywhere we are by our actions and words. Let us open wide those areas in our lives which until now have been sealed from the King. We must seek the Lord relentlessly until He responds to our cry and earnest longing. Let us seek Him while He is available, while we can find Him. Let us seek Him while He is still willing to hear us and respond to our call.

It is time to forsake our sins and compromises. It is time to "come out and be separate" from a world that seems to have squeezed us into its mold. It is time to abandon our own ways, methods and schemes and return to the power of the Holy Spirit. Let us abandon our low standards and embrace the standards of God.

Let us forsake our love of pleasure and frivolity and be committed to the business of the King. Let us forsake all thoughts of self-sufficiency that take our hearts away from Him. Let us forsake all thoughts of self-exaltation, of giving up the race and retreating from the battle ground. Let us turn to Him with all our heart, all our soul, and all our strength.

We must turn to Him with all that we are and have if we want a response. Let us cry for mercy and deliverance from misery, poverty, blindness and nakedness. Let us turn to Him in response to His counsel that we buy from Him "Gold refined in the fire" so that we can become rich, spiritually, emotionally, psychologically and physically. Yes, so that we can become rich in God.

Let us buy from Him "white clothes to wear", so as to cover our shameful nakedness. Let us clothe ourselves with His righteousness that we walk through this world in white. Let us turn to Him for the purification of our eyes so that we can see our hopelessness without His presence, our uselessness without His power, and cling to Him. Like the beloved in the Song of Songs, we have spent the night without the lover. It is time for us to get up and search for the One our hearts love. We must put in all we have in seeking Him, until we find Him.

HOW DO WE SEEK HIM?

"... and that He rewards those who earnestly seek Him" (Hebrew 11:6).

"But if from there you seek the Lord your God, you will find Him if you look for Him with all your heart and with all your soul" (Deuteronomy 4:29).

If we are to seek God, our seeking Him must be marked by deep conviction. We must be convinced that, it is Him we need at such a time as this. We must painstakingly seek Him if we ever expect Him to reward our search with a revelation of Himself. Seeking God must be with our whole heart (spirit) which implies that our intuition, communion and conscience must all be involved in the search. We must seek Him with our whole soul which implies that our mind must be actively involved, our will must be involved and our emotions must also be involved.

It means we must think of him often and allow our mind to focus on Him. Our will must be engaged in a firm resolve to find Him. Whatever distracts you emotionally from seeking Him must be ruthlessly dealt with. Whatever distracts your mind from focusing on Him must be overthrown. Whatever divides your devotion and attention to Him must be forsaken. These are just some practical implications involved in a diligent search for God.

WHY MUST WE RETURN?

"Come, let us return to the LORD. He has torn us to pieces but he will heal us; he has injured us but he will bind up our wounds. After two days he will revive us; on the third day he will restore us, that we may live in his presence. Let us acknowledge the LORD; let us press on to acknowledge him. As surely as the sun rises, he will appear; he will come to us like the winter rains, like the spring rains that water the earth" (Hos 6:1-3).

We have said that we must return to God through a diligent search for Him. Here we present reasons why we must return to the Lord.

FOR HEALING

Today's church is bruised, wounded, broken and injured as a result of schisms. The question God is asking us is *"why should you be beaten anymore? Why do you persist in rebellion? Your whole head is injured, your whole heart afflicted. From the sole of your foot to the top of your head, there is no soundness – only wounds and welts and open sores, not cleansed or bandaged or soothed with oil"* (Isa 1:5,6).

Shall we not return to Him wholeheartedly so as to be healed? Don't we need healing as individuals - Physical, emotional, psychological, financial, and above all, spiritual healing? Don't we need healing as families? Are there not broken homes or broken relationships that must be mended by His love and power? Do we not need healing as a church from our backslidden and fallen standards? Are we not in need of healing of our spiritual blindness and lack of vision? Are we not in need for healing from consciences that are deadened with respect to the needs of the world? Are we not in need of healing from our moral failures? We must return to God for healing if we must maximize the few minutes we have left. '… he has torn us to pieces but he will heal us" if we return to Him.

> *We need the rain of God to pour down in mighty torrents and wash away the debris littered all over the church. May it come and sweep away every trace of disdain in the church so that every faulty foundation will crumble and be swept away by the river of God's Spirit.*

FOR REVIVAL:

"After two days he will revive us"

If there is one thing which will take us out of the mire in which we have placed ourselves, it is revival, a complete reawakening to the standards and values of true Christianity. It is a reawakening to the consciousness of the sovereignty and centrality of Christ in the church and in our lives as individuals. That is what we need at such a time as this. A reawakening to wholehearted devotion and following of the Master!

We need the rain of God to pour down in mighty torrents and wash away the debris littered all over the church. May it come and sweep away every trace of disdain in the church so that every faulty foundation will crumble and be swept away by the river of God's Spirit. The Lord has promised that He will "make rivers flow on barren heights and springs within the valleys" and "turn the desert into pools of water, and the parched ground into springs" (Isa 41:18). That is His promise but we must return to Him if we are to experience it.

For the wise and discerning person, everything around is pointing to the need for revival, and there is every indication that it will come. God wants to pour out His Spirit upon His people; He wants to do a new thing in His church. The wise will do everything to cooperate with God in response to the call to prepare the way for this mighty outpouring of the Spirit. The harbinger of the Messiah, John the Baptist cried out,
"Prepare the way for the Lord; make straight paths for him. Every valley shall be filled in, every mountain and hill made low. The crooked roads shall become straight, the rough ways smooth. And all mankind will see God's salvation" (Luke 3:4-6).

There are basically two things that hinder the visitation of God
1) Sin cherished by an individual and the church
2) Idols in the heart (Eze 14:3)

This is the time to call sin by its name and forsake it. It is time to begin the Josiah kind of reforms in our lives as individuals and the church as a body. (See 2 Chronicles 34). You must cut down the altars of Baal in your life; you must cut to pieces the incense altars. It is time to smash the asheral poles. These represent what is keeping you from God's presence. It will surely be a painful process yet it is indispensable for revival.

The cry is that you make straight paths for Him. This means you must align your interests with His and you must align your delights with His. In the passage in Hosea it says we must <u>acknowledge Him</u> and press on to acknowledge Him. This means we have to accept His workings in our lives. We must submit to His Lordship and give ourselves totally to Him. We must say, "deal with me as thou seest meet". We must press on i.e. be determined, exercising some importunity. As we prepare His way and make straight His paths, He will come to us like a pent up flood.

When we prepare His way and He comes, the vacuum of inconsistencies and unfaithfulness in our lives shall be filled. The mountains and hills, significant of the difficulties raised by Satan shall be made low. We have tried to win the battle on our own, no doubt the defeats! When revival comes, we can stand and see the victory the Lord will bring. When we do our part, God does His. His purpose is to reveal His glory to all mankind and that can only be done through you and me. When the world sees that God is with us, when they behold His glory on us, then they will come running to us as the word says:

> *"Arise, shine, for your light has come, and the glory of the LORD rises upon you. See, darkness covers the earth and thick darkness is over the peoples, but the LORD rises upon you and his glory appears over you. Nations will come to your light, and kings to the brightness of your dawn"* (Isa 60:1-3).

We have tried to win people over by our human mechanism and techniques, therefore failure has been evident. God has a better plan for us, that of the people seeing His glory over the church. To emphasis on this point read 2 Chronicles 14 and 15. The reforms carried out by king Asa brought about the restoration of the presence of God in Judah, and consequently his victory over the enemies of his kingdom.

Do you see the need? Will you begin preparing His way? In the words of Azariah "...be strong and do not give up, for your work will be rewarded" (2 Chronicles 15:7). Yes, your work of preparing the way of the Lord will be rewarded if you do not give up. My focus on 2 Chronicles 14 and 15 is verse 9b, which says, "… For large numbers had come over to him from Israel when they saw that the Lord his God was with him".

We have struggled in vain to win people to the Lord but as soon as revival comes and God's favor, glory, and presence are evident among His people, large numbers of unbelievers will abandon their sinful ways and come over to the winning side. They shall abandon their waywardness and rebellion and submit to the King. Let us go in for revival, which is the need of our time.

> *This is the time to call sin by its name and forsake it. It is time to begin the Josiah kind of reforms in our lives as individuals and the church as a body.*

THE BENEFITS OF REVIVAL

We have mentioned some of the benefits of revival; now let us put them together in a comprehensive manner

1. Overcoming personal weakness, failures and inconsistencies; "Every valley shall be filled in".

2. Overcoming Satan's resistance; "Every mountain and hill made low".

3. Mass soul winning. "For large numbers had come over to him from Israel when they saw that the Lord his God was with him".

The next set of points will come from Isaiah 41:19, *"I will put in the desert the cedar and the acacia, the myrtle and the olive. I will set pines in the waste land, the fir and the cypress together..."*

We shall bring out the benefits as we examine the above verse in detail.

The cedar is a magnificent, firmly rooted, strong evergreen tree. It does not decay quickly and it is an insect repellant. Thus when revival comes,

4. There will be fruitfulness, fruit that abides. The fruit of repentance, the fruit of the Spirit, and the fruit of evangelism.

5. There will be durability in the effects of our works and prayers.
6. Revival will drive away the pests in your life. It will repel sickness and disease. Sin will be uncomfortable around you and will flee your presence. Sinners in the church will either repent or be repelled.

The acacia wood was used to construct the Ark of the Covenant and the Tabernacle which were significant of the presence of God amongst His people. It produces gum used as adhesives; it is medicinal and is used in producing dyes. Thus when revival comes,

7. God's presence will be established amongst us. He shall enable us to turn visitations to habitation in our lives as individuals and the church as a body.

8. There will be unity amongst God's people. Just as the gum is used to hold things together, so revival will hold the church together. Where things have not been holding together in

individual lives, homes, families and even nations, revival will cause things to hold together. It is not unity that brings revival but revival that brings unity.

9. There will be healing of individuals and whole communities of people; emotional, physical, psychological and spiritual healing.

10. There will be distinction, beauty and attractiveness. The dye is used to provide coloring for beauty and attraction. Again because things are distinguished by their colors, the church will stand distinct from the world, the believer will distinguish himself wherever he is in whatever he does. The beauty of God will rest upon each child of God.

The myrtle is a plant that produces fragrant flowers with spicy-sweet scented leaves. It is used as a symbol for peace and prosperity. Thus when revival comes,

11. It will bring meaning and sweetness to our daily lives. Our daily living will produce life-giving aroma as we mingle with others.

12. There will be peace and prosperity in our lives as individuals, in homes and families, in the church as a body and why not nations. Revival brings about prosperity of man; spirit, soul and body.

The olive plant produces olive oil which is of economic importance. Olive oil was used to keep the lamp of His presence burning. It is used for anointing the sick. Thus when revival comes,

13. There will be abundant revelation from God to individuals and to the church: revelation of our inheritance in Him, and revelation of strategies for victory.

14. The anointing of God will rest upon His church for effective service and ministry. People will be delivered from all bad habits, bondages, and diseases because anointing breaks the yoke.

15. The pine exemplifies peace, prosperity and reconciliation to God. Thus when revival comes. People will seek reconciliation with God. Peace with God will become foremost in people's minds. The ministry of reconciliation which God has given us will flourish as multitudes will turn to God and become an active part of it. (2 Cor. 15:18-21).

16. The fir is used as an emblem of nobility and great stature. Thus when revival comes the church shall be held in high esteem and regard by outsiders. The dignity of the believer will become evident and we shall influence the world and not the other way round.

17. The cypress is a tall reddish-hued wood. Thus when revival comes, we shall be strong and robust. We shall be able to resist every onslaught of the enemy. We shall be bold, fearless, and courageous to face the uncertain.

These are the benefits of revival to individuals, homes, communities, and the church.

FOR RESTORATION

The third reason for which we must return is for restoration: "On the third day He will restore us". If we are to be restored to Bible standards then we must return to God. Let us return that He may restore us to His heart. Let us return that He may restore our true values and worth. Let us return that He may restore our lost dignity and respect. Let us return that He may restore us to our rightful place of power and influence.

> "Restore us, O Lord God Almighty; make your face shine upon us, that we may be saved" (Ps 89:19).

We must plead, desperately plead, with the Almighty to restore us to Himself and to restore our rightful inheritance in Him. We must show signs of earnest desperation for this restoration. We must understand that without this restoration the effects of the coming revival will not last for long. However, restoration will not take only pleading. There are practical things which must be done.

> *"But if you will look to God and plead with the Almighty, if you are pure and upright, even now he will rouse himself on your behalf and restore you to your rightful place. Your beginnings will seem humble, so prosperous will your future be"*(Job 8:5-7).

1. LOOKING UP TO GOD:
"But if you will look to God..."

If we must be restored, then we must come to a point where "all our eggs are placed in one basket," the basket of God. We must come to a point where we look up to no other thing but God, where all our hopes and trust are no longer on our schemes and methods but on God. We must come to a point where we look to God alone for results. We must look to Him alone for our sustenance and empowerment. We must come to a point where we will say "without you we are done" and "unless thou bless me I must die".

2. SUPPLICATION:
"and plead with the Almighty"

Restoration is not a right but a favour. The prodigal son understood that he was not worthy to be restored to the position of a son, but the father's rich generosity brought him once more to that position. That is favour. We too must plead with God to restore us to Himself and to our rightful place.

3. SANCTIFICATION:
"If you are pure and upright…"
"Wash your hands, you sinners, and purify your hearts, you who are double-minded (Jas $3:8^b$).

Thirdly, if we must be restored we must throw away all our sins and idols. We must purify our hearts and lives through true repentance and restitution where need be. We must make up our minds to go in for restoration come what may.

> When all this is done, God will rouse Himself on our behalf and restore us to our rightful place. He will rouse Himself on your behalf and restore your vision, your health, your finances, your relationships, your strength and courage, your joy, your peace, and your honor.

CHAPTER TEN

A TIME FOR DISTINCTION

God's call to His church has always been, "therefore come out from them and be separate" (2 Cor 6:17). His will has always been that there be a clear demarcation between the world and the church. This was evident in the early church as written in the Acts of the Apostles:

"The apostles performed many miraculous signs and wonders among the people. And all the believers used to meet together in Solomon's Colonnade. No one else dared join them, even though they were highly regarded by the people" (Acts 5:12-13).

When the believers gathered, it was evident that the children of God had gathered. There was no mixture, no adulteration. People respected the holy Assembly of God's people. The church was held in high esteem and regard by all the people around. The evidence of miraculous signs and wonders showed that God's presence was among the saints each time they gathered. It was not a social club that anyone would join at any time.

For "...no one dared join them." That is the testimony of the early church. The church was distinct even though she was in the midst of non-believing Jews and Gentiles. This distinction, esteem and regard brought about the addition of those who believed in the Lord (V14). There was no joining (of those who had not believed) but there was a clear and daily addition to their numbers of those who believed in the Lord. That was the situation of the early church.

Can you compare and contrast the situation in today's church with that of the early church? There is nothing but a mixture of believers and unbelievers. Increasingly people who have not believed are joining the ranks of believers with no desire to change. They are looking for social clubs and religious shelter to cover their sin and wickedness. The church in her lack of power and the convicting presence of God has provided, for a long time now, just the right atmosphere for these unconverted among God's people.

Am I saying too much? Are many churches not just a mass of those who have a form of godliness but deny its power; its power to save from sin and to enable one live a pure and holy life? We have abandoned the message of salvation and repentance and have filled our sermons with "God bless you in your sin" slogans and clichés. We have given the people an impression that they can still keep their sins and make heaven as long as their names are written in some church register.

I wonder if the church registers have become the Lamb's Book of life! The world has increasingly laid its grip on the church and it is difficult, if not impossible in most cases, to make any distinction between the believer and the unbeliever, between those who fear God and those who do not, between those who serve Him and those who do not.

GOD'S COMMITMENT:

"And you will again see the distinction between the righteous and the wicked, between those who serve God and those who do not" (Mal 3:18).

The Bible says, "The Lord knows those who are his" (2 Ti 2:19) but He wants to make it known to the whole world. He wants to make a clear distinction between the saint and sinner, between the righteous and the wicked, between the believer and unbeliever. He understands and sees that the world has squeezed itself into the church. He knows that His house is a mixture of fake and genuine and He is committed to bring about a two-fold distinction. The time is coming, and has now come for a distinction between
- *God pleasers* and *men pleasers*
- Those who serve God and those who serve themselves
- Those who love the truth and those who hate it
- Those who are sincere and those who pretend
- Those who hold to godly standards and those who compromise.
- Those who are devoted, wholeheartedly committed to Him and those with divided hearts.
- Those who are committed to the will of God and those who do not bother.
- The upright in heart and the corrupt
- The true and the false
- Those who love the Lord and those who do not
- Those who fear Him and those who do not.

The Lord expects all who profess His Name to be committed to truth; in their desires, choices, delights, expenditure, use of time, speech etc. He expects all who profess His Name to be wholeheartedly commitment to obey the Lord.

A wholehearted commitment to honesty, truth and integrity!
A wholehearted commitment to live under the complete influence of the Holy Spirit!
A wholehearted commitment to the power of the Holy Spirit!
A wholehearted commitment to present one's best and all to Him!
A wholehearted commitment to holiness and righteousness!
A wholehearted commitment to total separation from the world!
A wholehearted commitment to the will of God!
A wholehearted laying down of one's rights and privileges on the altar of the Gospel of Christ. This is what God expects of us and His Spirit is there to work it in us.

SEPARATING THE RANKS

"Now when he saw the crowds, he went up on a mountainside and sat down. His disciples came to him, and he began to teach them, saying" (Matt 5:1-2).

The Lord Jesus was never interested in having the crowds follow Him. He wanted those who had decided to follow Him at any cost. Here He decided to separate them by climbing a mountain. When He did this, the Bible says, "His disciples came to Him..." In the crowd there was a mixture of disciples and non-disciples alike but the disciples were committed to follow at any length. The deep teachings given in the rest of the chapter were to His disciples. He carried out further separation even amongst His disciples by the things He taught.

It is written, "On hearing this many of His disciples said, 'This is a hard teaching, who can accept it? ... From this time many of His disciples turned back and no longer followed Him" (John 6:60-66). The teaching He gave here (cf. John 6) was with the goal of making a distinction between those who believed in everything He taught and those who chose what to believe; between those who had received a revelation of Him and those who just followed others, knowing not where they were going. Today He is making the same distinction and it will be evident to all.

> *The Lord Jesus was never interested in having the crowds follow Him. He wanted those who had decided to follow Him at any cost.*

WHAT BLOCKS VISION?

Why are there many people in the church without any vision? Why are there so many without any clear sight of the Savior and of what He wants them to do? It is because of an unholy contentment with life in the crowd. Many are contented staying amongst the masses, because of unholy and unnecessary attachments.

"Jesus entered Jericho and was passing through. A man was there by the name of Zacchaeus; he was a chief tax collector and was wealthy. He wanted to see who Jesus was, but being a short man he could not, because of the crowd. So he ran ahead and climbed a sycamore-fig tree to see him, since Jesus was coming that way" (Luke 19:1-4).

It seems many brethren in the church long to see the Savior in His beauty and glory. They seem to pray sincerely, "O Lord open my eyes that I may see you" but fail to realize that, the Lord is not hiding from them. He longs to reveal Himself more than we long to behold Him. What blocks your view of Him is the crowd. What acts as impediment to your vision is the crowd. Because of this crowd in which you have placed yourself you cannot have any clear vision or purpose in life. It diminishes the clarity of whatever you see if at all you see anything.

If you are desperate for a vision, you must come out of the crowd. You must run ahead of those around you. There must be a clear distinction from the ordinary with respect to your pursuit of the Savior. You must get to a height above your peers so you can see clearly. This will take painful climbing of your own sycamore. It will mean despising the shame that may be involved. It will mean taking the risk to climb. It will mean the pain of a lonely waiting on the sycamore. But you have got to be desperate for that vision.

> *If you are desperate for a vision, you must come out of the crowd. You must run ahead of those around you. There must be a clear distinction from the ordinary with respect to your pursuit of the Savior. You must get to a height above your peers so you can see clearly.*

You cannot have it by continuously mingling and staying in the crowd that blocks your view. Be willing to sacrifice the comfort of the crowd, the approval of the crowd, the warmth and security of the crowd. Your crowd may just be friends, it may just be your family, and it may be your job or business. It may be an established system which will not permit you to do that which God has put in your heart to do for Him.

For Abraham, it was his family, and so God told him, "Leave your country, your people and your father's household and go to the land I will show you" (Gen 12:1). If Abram had to see the land, he had to leave. However because his separation was not complete, he could not have a clear vision of what God wanted him to see. In my book "Fulfilling your Destiny" I wrote,

> "There must be a breaking free from ties to mediocrity and purposelessness for God to work with us and through us. There must be a breaking free from failures of the past. There must be a breaking free from traditions and customs and people who can hinder one's purpose:
> 1. Those who have no vision and are not bothered. These are people whose lives are committed to nothing, whose only reason for living is because they were born and whose only goal is to continue a lineage. Such people can never be an inspiration to you.
> 2. Those who failed and gave up;
> These are people who once had a vision and were committed to it but later gave it up. Such will see it impossible to accomplish anything. I do not mean those who failed but are making use of their failures to continue their pursuit. Such people are great resources.
> 3. The customs and believes and traditions and ways of those who have no purpose.
> 4. The customs, believes, traditions, ways and mind-sets of those who failed and gave up.
> 5. The things and people who can be of no consequence to a purposeful life.

Unless there is this necessary separation, there can be no way to see what God wants to show you.
This was exactly the case with Abram. Though he left his country and father's household, he did not separate from his people. The Bible says, "…so Abram left, as the LORD had told him; and Lot went with him" (Gen 12: 4a).

From then on, Lot was a barrier to Abram's vision, and as such he couldn't see clearly what the Lord had to show him. Every tie, anything we cling to, from which we ought to separate will only act as a hindrance to our purpose.

Though Abram, was now in Canaan he could not receive further light because he had not fully obeyed the separation command. Because God had a greater purpose for Abram, He brought about a circumstance, which caused him to be separated from Lot.

God will create circumstances to separate you from all you are clinging to, which is unnecessary to the accomplishment of your vision.

> The LORD only gave Abram further light and method of accomplishment when his separation from Lot was effected."

A CALL TO THE MOUNTAIN

> *"As soon as they had brought them out, one of them said, "Flee for your lives! Don't look back, and don't stop anywhere in the plain! Flee to the mountains or you will be swept away!"*
>
> *But Lot said to them, "No, my lords, please! Your servant has found favor in your eyes, and you have shown great kindness to me in sparing my life. But I can't flee to the mountains; this disaster will overtake me, and I'll die. Look, here is a town near enough to run to, and it is small. Let me flee to it; it is very small, isn't it? Then my life will be spared."*
>
> *He said to him, "Very well, I will grant this request too; I will not overthrow the town you speak of. But flee there quickly, because I cannot do anything until you reach it" (That is why the town was called Zoar)"* (Gen 19:17-22).

The story of Sodom and Gomorrah is a familiar one to many who grew up with a Christian background. This brief overview of the story is for those who may not be familiar with it.

Lot the nephew of Abraham had separated from his uncle after choosing the best part of the land as he (Lot) saw it. He later found himself amongst a people who practiced all sorts of perversion the human mind can conceive. The Bible says their wickedness and the outcry against them had reached the throne of God Almighty (Gen 18:20) who decided to do something about it. The Sovereign LORD sent two of His angels to investigate the situation and decide on what to do concerning the cities.

Following what the angels saw, their decision was to have the cities destroyed. However, they were to spare Lot's life and the lives of those related to him because he was found righteous. It is just amazing how God's grace brought them (Lot, his wife and two daughters) out of the city. When they were brought safely out of the city, the instruction given them was "Flee for your lives! Don't look back, and don't stop anywhere in the plain! Flee to the mountain or you will be swept away!"

From the above verse, we can outline the following clearly spelt out instructions.
1. Flee for your lives
2. Don't look back
3. Don't stop anywhere in the plain
4. Flee to the mountains.

To flee is to run in the most undignified, uncalculated manner. God has asked us to "flee from sexual immorality" (1 Cor 6:18) and to "flee the evil desires of youth" (2 Ti 2:22) but it seems to me, many have decided to ignore these instructions to their own undoing. Many play with immoral music, movies, dressing, and companionship, and in the process they have destroyed themselves. They have decided to tread where angels have not dared to and have reaped bitter consequences. My dear, you have to flee when it comes to youthful passions and sexual immorality. Do not try to resist, the Bible recommends that you flee, no two ways!

The second instruction you have been given in order for you to effectively run this race is "Don't look back". This is because looking back slows you down, it makes you lose focus on the finishing point and obstacles on way. The Lord Jesus Christ said, "No one who puts his hand to the plough and looks back is fit for the service in the kingdom of God". (Like 9:62) Looking back disqualifies you for service in God's kingdom.

Do you long for the things you abandoned in Egypt? Do you long for the garlic and cucumbers and spices you once abandoned in response to God's call on your life? Are you looking and longing for the help that comes from Egypt? Then you simply disqualify yourself from service in His Kingdom. Many, like Lot's wife, who have failed to heed this warning, have become spiritual pillars of salts, useless in the household of God.

The plain signifies nothing but mediocrity, the ordinary and the natural. It depicts the place of worldly comfort, ease, and compromise. God does not expect you to live your Christian life in mediocrity, like any ordinary man will. He wants you to move to the mountain - the place of the supernatural, the place of the extraordinary and the place of excellence.

MOUNTAIN TOP IS YOUR HOME

You are destined for the mountain top and not the plain. Do not get accustomed to the mediocre lifestyle. That will mean you living far below what God destined you for. However, to get to the mountain top, there are no elevators, no one carries another; you have to climb to where God wants you to be. Now this is just where the trouble is. We have been so accustomed to having things the easy way, and so people are afraid to climb to the mountain top the right way. Increasingly, as time passes, many more seem to tell God they are contented staying in the plain.

Fear to climb your mountain is the beginning of failure. Resigning to mediocrity is the curse that has plagued humankind. You are where you are because of your personal choice to climb to the top or to stay at the foot of that mountain. Lot's failure and eventual destruction began when he decided to negotiate with God. "But Lot said, No my Lord, please!" Religion is calling Christ Lord and in the same breath saying "no" to His commands. Lot said "Lord" and at the same time he said "No" to a command from his "Lord". Is that not the plight of the church today? So many people are willing to call Him Lord but still live in flagrant disobedience to spiritual and biblical teachings. God have mercy on us!

God is building a church – an army of people – that is willing to do what He says and to go where He sends. The negotiator has no spiritual future. The negotiator will go nowhere and will rise to nothing. The negotiator is automatically disqualified. God is building a people who at any given time are ready to say "I can do all things" not those who like Lot can only say "I can't". God wants those who know that with Him they can make the impossible to happen, who can say "though I walk through the valley of the shadow of death, I fear no evil" not those who say, "this disaster will overtake me, and I will die"

Have you resolved to live on the plain or on the mountain? The plain is the place of compromise with sin and the world. It is the place of human traditions and religion. On the other hand, the mountain is the place of experience with God; it is the place of the supernatural and excellence. Why does God want us to get to the mountain?

Fear to climb your mountain is the beginning of failure. Resigning to mediocrity is the curse that has plagued humankind. You are where you are because of your personal choice to climb to the top or to stay at the foot of that mountain.

-To receive instruction (see Ex 19:3, 20). God wants to give you instruction for fruitful and effective living.

-To view the Promise Land (see Deuteronomy 34:1). God wants to give you a glimpse of what He has in store for you, so as to stir your faith.

-To intercede (see Ex. 17:9). God has a prayer assignment for you, and you can only carry it out on the mountain.

-To transfer authority (see Numbers 20:25-26). Just as Aaron's authority was transferred to Eleazar, so authority will flow from the throne to you on the mountain.

-To commune with God (see I Kings 19:11). The mountain is a place for a God encounter.

-To receive revelation (see Matt 17:1). There are things which can only be revealed to those who have climbed the mountain.

The mountain is the place of *aloneness* with God, the place of a complete one-on-one dealing with the God of the universe. It is the place where a man confronts his life viz-a-viz the demands of the cross.

OVERCOME YOUR FEARS

The question can be asked, "...why are people afraid of the mountain?" There are several reasons, I believe, why many are contented with this mediocre spiritual lifestyle, among which are:

i) Failure to take God for His Word (V 19):
Just as Lot tried to negotiate with God instead of trusting Him and running, in faith, to the mountain, knowing that He who asked him to run to that mountain will be patient enough to wait until he reached the mountain, many today fail to exercise simple faith on the Word of God. They have brought in human reasoning and ideas into the simple heavenly commands. To experience life on the mountain, you must take God for His Word. Refuse to negotiate God's Word with circumstances and human philosophy.

ii) The tendency to belong (V 20):
Man always has this tendency to want to belong. Because life on the mountain will require some kind of separation from the crowd, separation from the ordinary, people tend to shun it. Life on the mountain will require you taking the journey alone to stand before your God. It may require staying alone in the presence of God for hours or days. Those who are bound by the love of the company of man automatically shun the mountain life. God wants you to be an eagle, ready to rise to the topmost height alone, not a chicken.
The next points will come from these two passages:

> *"LORD, who may dwell in your sanctuary? Who may live on your holy hill? He whose walk is blameless*

> *and who does what is righteous, who speaks the truth from his heart and has no slander on his tongue, who does his neighbor no wrong and casts no slur on his fellowman, who despises a vile man but honors those who fear the LORD, who keeps his oath even when it hurts, who lends his money without usury and does not accept a bribe against the innocent. He who does these things will never be shaken"* (Ps 15:1-5).

> *"Who may ascend the hill of the LORD? Who may stand in his holy place? He who has clean hands and a pure heart, who does not lift up his soul to an idol or swear by what is false"* (Ps 24:3-5).

iii)   Failure to walk blamelessly:

Failure to walk blamelessly before the Father and the watching world has made many afraid of life on the mountain. If we are to live on God's holy hill, if we are to dwell on His Mountain, then we must walk through this world in white, we must neither be tainted with sin nor compromise with worldly standards.

iv)   Falsehood:

Those who must live on the mountain are those who call white, white, and black, black. They are not afraid to speak the truth. Their hearts agree with what their lips declare. You must keep away from falsehood if you will climb the mountain.

v)   Slander:

It is impossible to speak against anyone with ill intent and then climb God's holy mountain. Uncleanness of the tongue disqualifies many from the mountain experience, for they are afraid of the cleansing flame from God's altar.

vi) Broken Promises:

Those who will dwell are bound by their words. They fulfill their promises. God wants you to be committed to what your lips proclaim, whether to Him or to a fellow man. Do you utter promises without any commitment to keep them?

vii) Greed:

The tendency to accumulate things even at the expense of others disqualifies many from the mountain life. No one ever climbs the mountain with increasing load. On the contrary, as he climbs, the load reduces. The greedy cannot experience life on God's holy mountain. Spiritual and moral excellence is far from them. What is your attitude towards money and material things? Do you desire more and more things? Do you derive satisfaction in life from the things you acquire?

viii) Unclean hands:

Are your hands clean? Have you used them to touch things you are not supposed to or to touch people in places you are not supposed to? Have you pointed maliciously at others? Have you stolen? Have you murdered?

Are your hands washed in the blood of the Lamb? Unless they be washed and cleansed you cannot live the mountain experience.

ix) Impure Hearts:

Is your heart free from unforgiveness? Is it free from resentment and despise? Is your heart free from malice and hypocrisy? Is it free from doubt and evil suspicion? Is it free from sexual sin?

Have you heed to the command to "purify your hearts"? Those who must dwell on the mountain have pure hearts and clean consciences. No one whose heart condemns him or is impure can feel comfortable on the holy mountain of God.

x)   Idolatry:

Has something taken God's place in your life? What has occupied the time you gave to God? What has replaced your devotion to the Kingdom? What has crowded your mind such that God no longer has a place there? What place does God occupy in your heart? Who has the final say in your daily affairs?

If you must dwell on the mountain, then you must rid your heart and life of anything that competes with the Lordship of Christ Jesus.

Will you respond, wholeheartedly and with an irrevocable yes, to the call for a mountain experience? Will you now abandon the comfort of the plain? More than ever, then the time is now. Like the Psalmist, with all urgency, it is time to cry out to God, "send forth Your light and Your truth, let them guide me; let them bring me to Your holy mountain, to the place where you dwell" (Ps 43:3). The prophet Isaiah also echoed what we have been saying here

> *"The sinners in Zion are terrified; trembling grips the godless: "Who of us can dwell with the consuming fire? Who of us can dwell with everlasting burning?" He who walks righteously and speaks what is right, who rejects gain from extortion and keeps his hand from accepting bribes, who stops his ears against plots of murder and shuts his eyes*
>
> *against contemplating evil; this is the man who will dwell on the heights, whose refuge will be the mountain fortress. His bread will be supplied, and water will not fail him. Your eyes will see the king in his beauty and view a land that stretches afar"* (Isa 33:14-17).

Life on the mountain is a blessed life!
Life on the mountain is a secured life!
Life on the mountain is one of constant supplies!
Life on the mountain is receives constant vindication from the Lord!

You have nothing to lose and everything to gain when committed to spiritual excellence. There is everything to gain when you decide to pay the price to live above mediocrity. If you are to impact your generation Godward then you must respond to the call to be distinct and refuse to get yourself squeezed into the mold of worldly compromise and fallen standards. Decide to be the eagle you were meant to be. You belong to the summit not to the foot of the mountain. You were meant to soar and not to crawl. Decide to become all God wants you to be.

Don't let sin steal any away!
Don't let the world deprive you of any!
Don't let the devil thwart any part of it!

CHAPTER ELEVEN

A TIME TO LIVE READY

Let us impact this world for the King and the Kingdom in this last hour. Let us muster all are and have; let us be totally involved in the business of the kingdom for maximum impact. This will be done, and done quickly, if we see the need to live ready. In the previous chapters we underscored the need to understand the times. We saw the urgency of the hour we live in.

We also saw the need to confront reality. We pointed out the urgent need to rebuild the foundations. We saw what our response must be, and the need to be distinct. I am writing this chapter having in mind that your heart has responded positively to what has been taught so far and that you are taking the necessary actions.

"Let us rejoice and be glad and give him glory! For the wedding of the Lamb has come, and his bride has made herself ready" (Rev 19:7).

LIVING READY IMPLIES SELF-EXAMINATION

"All a man's ways seem innocent to him, but motives are weighed by the Lord" (Pr 16:2).

To do something for the right reason is totally different from doing it for the wrong reason. As we do the business of the King, ensure that you are doing everything for the right reason and with the right motive – God's eternal Kingdom and glory.

The subtlety of sin and evil is far entrenched in our environment, and sad to say, in the hearts of professing believers. The Lord warned that "Because of the increase of wickedness, the love of most will grow cold" (Mt 24:12). Unfortunately, even with this coldness in love, man may still be involved in all kinds of seemingly profitable activism. It will not pay for you to continue in activities when the love for God in your heart has grown cold. It is time for you to constantly examine your heart in God's presence to know whether the love for God is still there.

This is what the Lord said to the church in Ephesus:
> *"To the angel of the church in Ephesus write:*
> *These are the words of him who holds the seven stars in his right hand and walks among the seven golden lampstands: I know your deeds, your hard work and your perseverance. I know that you cannot tolerate wicked men, that you have tested those who claim to be apostles but are not, and have found them false. You have persevered and have endured hardships for my name, and have not grown weary. Yet I hold this against you: You have forsaken your first love. Remember the height from which you have fallen! Repent and do the things you did at first. If you do not repent, I will come to you and remove your lampstand from its place"*
> (Rev 2:1-5).

- These people worked hard, extremely hard for the King and His kingdom.

- They persevered under hard times, trials and testing to keep their faith in the Lord.
- They had no place for the wicked.
- They were sensitive and could discern the false from the genuine
- They had not gone weary in spite of all they went through.

> *In the midst of such prevalent evil, wisdom demands that you cease from all activity and withdraw often, into God's presence, in order to listen to the voice of the Spirit. You need to be quiet and hear His words of approval or disapproval*

However, in the eyes of God they were regarded as people who had fallen from a great height because in all these they had forsaken their first love. In other words their love had grown cold. How hot is your love? This question can only be answered in the presence of God as His Spirit sheds light and understanding.

The need for self-examination cannot be over emphasized as God's word is not silent about it:

"A man ought to examine himself ... " (I Cor 11:28).

"Examine yourselves to see whether you are in the faith; test yourselves" (II Cor 13:5^a).

"Let us examine our ways and test them, and let us return to the Lord" (Lam 3:40).

When a man ought to do something, it talks of a duty, it talks of responsibility. Hence it is your duty or responsibility to examine yourself in the light of God's presence. Make sure you are doing everything for the right reason. The prophet Amos said. "Therefore the prudent man keeps quiet in such times, for the times are evil" (5:13).

In the midst of such prevalent evil, wisdom demands that you cease from all activity and withdraw often, into God's presence, in order to listen to the voice of the Spirit. You need to be quiet and hear His words of approval or disapproval. Do not allow yourself to get too busy such that you can't find time regularly to withdraw from the humdrum of society. That is the way to grow in love!

Is your love growing deeper, wider, stronger, brighter and firmer? Are you consumed by the zeal for His house? Are you passionate about the Savior and the Cross? How fervent is your love? You are commanded to "Never be lacking in zeal, but keep your spiritual fervor, serving the Lord" (Rom 12:11). Get up each morning with a renewed zeal. Let each day dawn with your heart set aflame for God, burning with the fragrance of an undying love for the risen Lord and soon coming King.

LIVING READY MEANS LIVING HOLY

We have been talking about the Lord's return from heaven soon. Those who are part of his church live in expectation to be raptured. This places on you the responsibility to live ready. At any one time you must be *rapturable*.

> *"Make every effort to live in peace with all men and to be holy; without holiness no one will see the Lord"* (Hebrews 12:14).

"Dear friends, now we are children of God, and what we will be has not yet been made known. But we know that when he appears, we shall be like him, for we shall see him as he is. Everyone who has this hope in him purifies himself, just as he is pure" (1 John 3:2-3).

> *Get up each morning with a renewed zeal. Let each day dawn with your heart set aflame for God, burning with the fragrance of an undying love for the risen Lord and soon coming King.*

Do you hope to see Him? Do you hope to be raptured when He comes to take His own to be with Him? Then it demands that you purify yourself and be holy. These are some parameters you can use to evaluate your holiness.

Is there passion in your heart for God?
Is there passion in your heart to know and understand the word of God?
Have you rid your heart of all sin?
Is your heart free from every trace of anger and unforgiveness?
Is there someone you cannot face and sincerely say "I love you, there is nothing in my heart against you?"
Are you living at peace with yourself?
Is there worry, anxiety and unrest in your heart?
Is your spirit perturbed within you over the cares of this life?

Do you give first place to the things and the people who deserve it?
Is your life irreversibly and irrevocably placed on the altar of God as a daily living sacrifice?

Is there fire in your heart that burns day and night and transforms the love and zeal in your heart into a sweet smelling aroma, pleasing to the Lord?
Do you awaken each morning with the longing to be taught, led, and directed by the Spirit of God?

To live holy means to be set apart for God. It demands being able to distinguish the sacred from the common, the pure from the impure, the holy from the unholy, the clean from the unclean. It may be at the level of motives, intents, thoughts, words or actions. Holiness means jealously guarding your heart from all that contaminates the body or spirit. It demands that you set up checkpoints to guard against everything suspicious. Holiness means maintaining the capacity to screen everything that enters your spirit.

What about sins which have become an "acceptable part of you" – sins that so easily beset? I have no other recommendation than what is found in the holy Book:
"Put to death, therefore, whatever belongs to your earthly nature: sexual immorality, impurity, lust, evil desires and greed, which is idolatry... But now you must rid yourselves of all such things as these: anger, rage, malice, slander, and filthy language from your lips. Do not lie to each other, since you have taken off your old self with its practices" (Col 3:5, 8-9).

One sure and steady way to put something to death is to cut off its supply of food. If you are to put your earthly nature to death, then you must stop feeding it. Sin is like a lion, no matter how strong and powerful it is, when there is nothing to feed on, it perishes. "The lion perishes for lack of prey, and the cubs of the lioness are scattered" (Job 4:11). No matter how monstrous the sin appears to be, no matter how deep it appears to have entrenched itself, if you cut off its supply, it will surely die. Sin only grows in power over the saint when you yield to its demands.

To be ready means to keep a short record of sin and to deal with it as soon as you are made aware by the Holy Spirit, through the Word, or through your conscience. It is ensuring that there's a clear line of communication between the Throne and your spirit so that you can be quick to respond to heaven's demands.

DISCONNECT THE SUPPLY

"Can papyrus grow tall where there is no marsh? Can reeds thrive without water? While still growing and uncut, they wither more quickly than grass" (Job 8:11-12).

Papyrus and reeds are plants which grow in marshes and serve as a hiding place for monsters (see Ps 68"30 and Job 40:21). Leviathan and Behemoth throughout scripture are figurative of Satan himself (see Job 41, Ps 74, Isa 27:1,2). Take away the marsh and the water from your life and the hiding place of Satan, the author of sin is taken away from your life. Sin will no longer find a hiding place in you. The marsh is figurative of thoughts, attitudes and tendencies which can easily lead to sin. Holiness demands that such be dealt with so that sin will cease to thrive.

> *Sin is like a lion, no matter how strong and powerful it is, when there is nothing to feed on, it perishes. "The lion perishes for lack of prey, and the cubs of the lioness are scattered" (Job 4:11).*

CHAPTER TWELVE

A TIME TO CROSS JORDAN

It appears the church has stood on the wilderness side of the Jordan for too long, contented with the provisional manna. We seem to have crossed the red sea but find ourselves wandering in the wilderness of failure, lack of vision and defeat. We have sent spies into the Promised Land who seem to have brought back reports that contentment with the wilderness experience is better than crossing the Jordan to fight for our inheritance.

However, there is every indication that now is time for the church of God to cross from the wilderness of spiritual poverty, impotence and mediocrity into the Christ-obtained, Blood-bought riches which are hers in Christ Jesus. All across the universe God is raising an army of prophets and priests, all carriers of His presence, who unitedly are stepping in the Jordan to stop the flow until all of God's people have crossed over into their inheritance.

Until now, the church has failed to occupy her Christ-ordained position, as Bride of the King of the Universe and has woefully failed to exercise her power of attorney because she still feels inferior. Why does she still feel inferior? Because she has failed to carry around the glory and aroma of her King! She has been contented with life in the wilderness. It is high time we all crossed the Jordan. I think more than ever before, the way has been cleared for all to cross over into the Promised Land. The wilderness has always been and will always be a place of failure, defeat, compromise and confusion. It will always be a place of *progress-less* motion. It will always be a place of the provisional.

We cannot afford to stay any longer in a place short of the best that God has for us. There is a call, for those who have ears to hear, going all across the globe that the priests are about to step into the Jordan, so everyone has to be ready. It is true that some, like the mighty men of David, have already crossed over even with the overflowing current. But it is time for even the weak and apparent feeble to cross over. Now let us turn to the Book and grab some nuggets from the narrative of the Israelites crossing over.

> *"Early in the morning Joshua and all the Israelites set out from Shittim and went to the Jordan, where they camped before crossing over. After three days the officers went throughout the camp, giving orders to the people: "When you see the ark of the covenant of the LORD your God, and the priests, who are Levites, carrying it, you are to move out from your positions and follow it. Then you will know which way to go, since you have never been this way before. But keep a distance of about a thousand yards between you and the ark; do not go near it." Joshua told the people "Consecrate yourselves, for tomorrow the LORD will do amazing things among you." Joshua said to the priests, "Take up the Ark of the Covenant and pass on ahead of the people." So they took it up and went ahead of them. And the LORD said to Joshua, "Today I will begin to exalt you in the eyes of all Israel, so they may know that I am with you as I was with Moses. Tell the priests who carry the Ark of the*

Covenant: 'When you reach the edge of the Jordan's waters, go and stand in the river" (Jos 3:1-8).

I want you to see that Joshua and all the Israelites were involved in this crossing over. It was not Joshua and some mighty men. It was not Joshua and the top commanders who crossed over. It was Joshua and all the Israelites. This is the time for even the baby Christians to cross over.

Now there is a mystery I want you to see here. Some Israelites had succeeded to settle on the east side of the Jordan. They had built tents for their families in an enclosed city. To man, we could have said part of Israel crossed over but the Holy Spirit says all Israel crossed over. This should teach us a profound lesson. Those who settle for anything other than the best God has, separate themselves from God's people. "Joshua and all the Israelites set out …" We must follow our Joshua – Jesus Christ into the fullness of the land the Father has assigned Him to allot to us.

> *All across the universe God is raising an army of prophets and priests, all carriers of His presence, who unitedly are stepping in the Jordan to stop the flow until all of God's people have crossed over into their inheritance.*

We must get into our spiritual fullness!
We must get into our financial fullness!
We must get into our material fullness!
We must get into our social fullness!
We must get into our physical fullness!

And these can only happen as we follow the lead of our Joshua – Jesus Christ. Reading the above passage in-depth, I want you to notice the following:

1. The Israelites set out from Shittim to Jordan.

Shittim was a place filled with acacia trees which had provided Israel with some kind of shelter in the wilderness. They had to move from this place of self-indulgence to the place of danger in order to confront their obstacles. God had to bring them closer to the Jordan so they could observe the magnitude of the flow of that great river and the potential disaster it could cause.

It is time for the church to come out of her hiding place of comfortable buildings, into the streets and confront the cries of the sick, destitute, possessed and all the others who desperately need her attention. Let us come out of our unholy indulgence in the shades of this world and confront that which stands before us as an impossible barrier into our Promised Land. It seems to me that God will always have us break camp from our comfort zones to where the real battle is.

The Israelites had to camp at the Jordan before crossing over. The word 'Jordan' comes from the Hebrew word Yardên, derived from Yârad which is a primary root, meaning to descend. For us to cross over our Jordan we must descend from our high and lofty Theology to the basic practical needs of dying humanity. We must bring down our philosophical strongholds and believe the simple Gospel of the cross and the Kingdom. We must camp at our Jordan to sink and subdue the machinery and mechanism of the enemy. That word also means to "get down".

Beloved, it is time we get down to practicalities; to see how we can make life a bit better for those around us. Let us get down and set free those in captivity to fear, sickness and diseases. Let us get down and liberate Satan's prisoners through the life-changing Gospel of the King and the Kingdom.

The word Yârad can also mean "to subdue". Until we begin exercising our dominion in this earth's realm given to us by God, many will continue to die in the wilderness. My friend, the wilderness is a hard and difficult place to live in, no matter what it offers as shelter and manna. The best for you lies in crossing the Jordan – the challenge of sin and the world into the Promised Land.
So what does Shittim represent to us?

(i) <u>The Place of Compromise</u>

"While Israel was staying in Shittim, the men began to indulge in sexual immorality with Moabite women, who invited them to the sacrifices to their gods. The people ate and bowed down before these gods. So Israel joined in worshiping the Baal of Peor. And the LORD's anger burned against them" (Numbers 25:1-3).

Shittim is the place of compromise with sexual immorality. Many people in the churches today are indulging with Moabite women and men. You must end all those illegal relationships no matter what they appear to offer you. Leave the Delilahs and the Jezebels before they kill you. Shittim is also the place of idolatry. Many people are worshipping the idol of money, fame, and materialism. Put an end to all your idolatry. There are others who feed from two tables; the table of demons and the table of the Lord. This should not, and can no longer exist in the church. Those who do not want to leave shittim will be purged out.
To cross your Jordan you must break camp and move from the place of compromise with any manner of sin. You must depart from the place of idolatry to the place where God is your All in all.

You must move from the place where God is angry with you to a place where you become a delight. My friend, you can't afford to spend another season at Shittim, now is the time for you to break camp.

(ii) <u>The Place of Defeat</u>

"...the valley of Shittim" (Joel 3:18^c KJV).

The valley represents the place of defeat and failure. It is the place where waste from the mountain is deposited. You can break camp and escape the defeats and failures of the past. You can rise from the darkness of the valley to the brightness of the mountain. Shittim is not the place for you. It is a place of defeated moral standards. It is a place where sin and the world triumph. My prayer for you is that you come out of Shittim now.
From 1Co. 6:7 we see the where there is defeat, there is also strife, bitterness, backbiting, malice, complaint, grumbling, murmuring etc.

(iii) <u>The Place Of Unbelief (doubt)</u>

"Then Joshua son of Nun secretly sent two spies from Shittim. "Go; look over the land," he said, "especially Jericho." So they went and entered the house of a prostitute named Rahab and stayed there" (Jos 2:1).

You know when the people camped at Shittim in Numbers 25:1 they did not move from there until Joshua 3:1. The Lord had promised to be with Joshua and to give him victory, but he decided to send spies to explore the land again. This was a result of doubt. He naturally depended on the external reports instead of what God had told him. You know, it was same with Gideon who only acted on the word when he heard the reports in the camp of the enemy.

Until men of God have labored with God to move their congregation from Shittim, there is no way their faith sermons can have impact in the life of their congregation. As long as a man or a woman remains in Shittim there is not much you can do to help them because they are inclined to the negative. You might give them all the good reports of the merits of the Promised Land and the grandeur of the God they serve but that will matter very little to them. Because Shittim is the place of doubt it is the place of lack and instability (see Jas 1:6-7).

When a man leaves Shittim, Jordan is only a brief stopover. Note that the Israelites spent just about a week camped at Jordan. After a man crosses Jordan the first place he or she camps at is Gilgal.

> "Remember (your journey) from Shittim to Gilgal, that you may know the righteous acts of the LORD" (Mic 6:5^b).

> "On the tenth day of the first month the people went up from the Jordan and camped at Gilgal on the eastern border of Jericho"(Jos 4:19).

Gilgal represents the place of circumcision, where the reproach of the flesh is taken away. The reason many people hesitate to cross the Jordan is because once the Jordan is crossed the flesh is dealt with. We are afraid of the knife and so forfeit the abundance that comes after that. My friend, it is time for you to move from Shittim - the place of compromise with sin, indulgence and unbelief, to Gilgal the place of circumcision of the heart, the place where the Spirit of God deals with your flesh, the place where you have faith in Him who has the knife that He will do a perfect job in your life. God wants to bring you to Gilgal, the place where you can begin tasting of God's goodness.

"Then the LORD said to Joshua, "Today I have rolled away the reproach of Egypt from you." So the place has been called Gilgal to this day.
On the evening of the fourteenth day of the month, while camped at Gilgal on the plains of Jericho, the Israelites celebrated the Passover. The day after the Passover, that very day, they ate some of the produce of the land: unleavened bread and roasted grain. The manna stopped the day after they ate this food from the land; there was no longer any manna for the Israelites, but that year they ate of the produce of Canaan"
(Jos 5:9-12).

> *The reason many people hesitate to cross the Jordan is because once the Jordan is crossed the flesh is dealt with. We are afraid of the knife and so forfeit the abundance that comes after that.*

Until we reach this point where God rolls away the reproach of our slavery to Satan, the reproach of our indulgence in sin and compromise with the World, God will not permit us taste of the produce of the land of promise. If the church must celebrate her Passover, she must cross her Jordan and reach Gilgal. Just four days after crossing Jordan, though they were still in pain as a result of the circumcision, they could celebrate the Lord's Passover. You cannot actually celebrate the Lord's Passover until the reproach of your past has been rolled away. And though Gilgal is a place of pain it is also the place of celebration and of blessing.

2. **The Priests had to take up their responsibility:**

The Priests, who were Levites, had to take up their responsibility to carry the Ark of the Covenant. They had to lift up on their shoulders the symbol of their covenant with God. In other words the only thing they were to carry at that time was the burden of their God. If we must cross our Jordan, we must "lay aside every weight" and carry with us the presence of God. It was impossible for those Priests carrying the ark to carry any other thing.

The Bible says "But you are a chosen people, a royal priesthood, a holy nation …" You belong to a community of *king-priests*. You must be a bearer of the covenant of your God. You must carry on you His presence if your Jordan has to make way for you. It is time to make use of the anointing of the royal priesthood and shake off any burden which is not of the Lord.

Why do many of us fail to function in the office of Priests? It is because we do not respect the terms of the priesthood. If we must function in the office of the priesthood, if we must flow in the anointing of this office, then God should be our only inheritance. We must be contented with Him as our all. Until God becomes enough for you, you cannot function in that anointing of the priesthood.

You must be united heart and soul with the High Priest – Jesus Christ (Heb 4:14). As you are united with Him, the anointing flows from Him down to you so you too can function under the unction of the priesthood.

Will you take up the intercessory role of the priesthood?
Will you take up the solution-providing role for the extension of God's Kingdom into a lost, needy and enslaved world? Oh Father,

cause the Priests, all over the world to take up their responsibility and extend your dominion to the common place of society. Let us carry the presence of our God wherever we go and provide solutions to the puzzles of life.

3. **The people had to move out of position:**

By this time the Israelites had moved out of Shittim and camped at the Jordan. Their camping here was not to be permanent, but God just wanted them to know the magnitude of the obstacle ahead of them. This new breed who did not experience the crossing of the red sea (except for a few whose parents had narrated the story to tthem) were to have a first class experience of the might of their God. Their camping at Jordan was only to bring them to the end of themselves, and unless God intervened their stay in the wilderness would be prolonged until the dry season.

The Lord God instructed them to move towards the Jordan even before the flow was stopped. They were to move and confront the obstacle in faith. Remember David had to move towards Goliath. It is time you and I move towards every Jordan standing on our way into God's promise for us as individuals. It is time we rise up and confront every Goliath. My brother, move out of your position of resignation and self-indulgence. It is time to move out of your position of unholy contentment with mediocrity. It is time you move out of your position of fear and anxiety towards faith and rest. Move out of your position of despair into hope and trust.

Like I said, Jordan was not to be permanent. We must move past the great obstacles into our individual Promised Land. It might take you forty years to reach there but it must not take you long to surmount that barrier. The Israelites camped at the Jordan for seven days approximately before crossing. You have observed the enemy for too long, confront him and get over that obstacle.

4. They had to follow the Ark

Although the people had to confront the obstacle, they had to follow the ark. They were not to follow their emotions, desires or fears but their focus had to be the Ark of the Covenant. They were only asked to follow the Priests who evidently were carrying the ark of the Lord. That was their only safety. If the Priests did not carry the ark, they were not to follow them.

There are many people demanding to be followed today. The wise heart understands the times we live in looks for the presence of one thing only - the Ark of the Covenant. If the one demanding a following is not evidently carrying upon his shoulders the ark of God's covenant, do not follow such a person. You will get lost in that wilderness or get drowned in the Jordan. The glory of God on a man or his ministry is what gives light. Do you want to know which way to go? You've got to follow nothing but the glory – the manifest presence of the King of heaven. Let us get into some details so as to help you recognize the presence of the ark in the life of a person.

> *"Behind the second curtain was a room called the Most Holy Place, which had the golden altar of incense and the gold-covered ark of the covenant. This ark contained the gold jar of manna, Aaron's staff that had budded, and the stone tablets of the covenant"* (Hebrews 9:3-4).

The ark contained basically three things; the gold jar of manna, Aaron's staff that had budded, and the stone tablets of the covenant. Let us see what each of these represents.

i. <u>The Gold Jar of Manna</u>

> *"So Moses said to Aaron; "Take a jar and put an omer of manna in it. Then place it before the LORD to be kept for the generations to come." As the LORD commanded Moses, Aaron put the manna in front of the Testimony, that it might be kept"* (Exodus 16:33-34).

This represents the supernatural ability of God to provide for His people. The manna was God's provision to His people in wilderness. The jar of manna was to be a testimony of God's kindness to the future generations. It was also symbolic of the power of our God to preserve that which can otherwise not be preserved. You remember the manna could not be kept overnight otherwise it would rot. But this one in the ark had to be there for generations to come. In a nutshell the gold jar of manna was representative of God's power to provide and to preserve. He provided for His people and He preserved them throughout their wilderness march.

Thus, to follow anyone, be sure that the source of his power, finances and authority is God. Prayerfully seek God about it.

ii. <u>Aaron's Staff That Had Budded:</u>

> *"The LORD said to Moses, "Put back Aaron's staff in front of the Testimony, to be kept as a sign to the rebellious. This will put an end to their grumbling against me, so that they will not die"* (Numbers 17:10).

There must be an evidence of the transforming power of God in the life of the one you are following. Remember Aaron's staff had been transformed in God's presence where it budded, blossomed, and produced almonds (Numbers 17:8). You have to look for the evidence of the resurrection life. You must look for the presence of the fruit of the Spirit and the character of the Lord Jesus. When a plant buds, blossoms and bears fruits, it is not for the plant but for others. Be sure the person is not involved in the building of a personal kingdom. Personal kingdoms can only be built at the expense of His Kingdom.

> *The gold jar of manna was representative of God's power to provide and to preserve. He provided for His people and He preserved them throughout their wilderness march.*

This staff was to be a symbol to the rebellious; hence you must be sure that the person you follow has also submitted himself to spiritual authority. Run away from anyone who is his own beginning and his own end. In other words keep away from all that will blind you to God's Justice. God will not spare anyone who grumbles against or usurps authority. Remember Korah and all his followers were destroyed. Never stand for or follow a rebellious cause, especially when it comes to spiritual authority. Watchman Nee treats this subject in greater detail in his book "Spiritual Authority".

iii. <u>The Stone Tablets</u>

"At that time the LORD said to me, "Chisel out two stone tablets like the first ones and come up to me on the mountain. Also make a wooden chest. I will write on the tablets the words that were on the first tablets, which you broke. Then you are to put them in the chest... Then I came back down the mountain and put the tablets in the ark I had made, as the LORD commanded me, and they are there now" (Deut 10:1-2, 5).

The stone tablets had on them the laws of God by which the people had to live. It was the law of God's covenant with them. It represented the holiness and righteousness of God. If you are to follow anyone you must be sure that he believes in the absolute authority of God's written word. Be sure that God's word is given its rightful place in his life and ministry. Be sure that God's righteousness and holiness are upheld by his life and message.

You must look for all the three components above. When they are evident, then you can wholeheartedly follow, in spite of the failures and weaknesses of the individual involved. God has not called you to only follow perfect people, you will never find any.

> *Many people today demand a following; to follow anyone look for evidences that he or she carries the presence of God, of the transforming power of the cross ,and that God's word takes centre stage in his or her life and ministry*

5. <u>They were to keep a distance between them and the ark.</u>

This was a warning to the Israelites that familiarity with the glory of God or with those carrying that glory is forbidden. You should be intimate with the glory of God or with those carrying that glory but never become familiar. Familiarity breeds presumption and disrespect. It is very dangerous to become familiar with a man who carries the glory. You can be intimate but that respect and esteem must be there.

It is time the church purges out every manner of familiarity with the Word of God, servants of God etc. Those who must cross their Jordan must respect this principle. This respect and esteem is not for the people per se, it is for the glory they are carrying. But because you cannot separate the glory bearer from the glory you just must esteem them in order for you to enter the land of promise.

Refuse and reject all forms or manifestations or tendency to become familiar. Treat familiarity as you would a viper. As soon as you see its ugly head do not hesitate to crush it.

6. <u>The People Had To Consecrate Themselves:</u>

Those who must cross the Jordan are those who have consecrated themselves to the Lord; those who have been separated and set apart for God and for his glory. Consecration implies separation from the common, the unclean and the unholy. It implies embracing all that is pure, clean and holy. You must set yourself apart for God and His kingdom, and then you will see the amazing things God will do in you, for you, and through you. This means separation from the wrong company and all that links you to the past.

7. The Priests had to Demonstrate Faith, Boldness and Sacrifice:

The Priests were to step into the water even before the flow stopped. This was a demonstration of faith and Spirit-inspired boldness. They were willing to take the risk of being swept away. One thing is sure; they understood that no flood waters can sweep away one who is carrying on him the glory of God. This caused the floodwaters to stop when they step in. They had faith in the God who had spoken and believed the prophet through whom He spoke. It is high time the church began to demonstrate faith and holy boldness.

Also the priest had to stand in the Jordan until every other person had crossed over. They were to stand there no matter how long it took. This is nothing but sacrifice. You must be willing to stand and help others cross their Jordan into the Land of Promise. You can stand with someone through prayer, a fast or financial support. O, that God will raise many such priests in our generation. Every step above is absolutely necessary for you to cross your Jordan. Anyone lacking will mean you remaining at or returning to shittim.

> *Familiarity breeds presumption and disrespect. It is very dangerous to become familiar with a man who carries the glory. You can be intimate but that respect and esteem must always be there.*

CHAPTER THIRTEEN

A TIME TO GIVE BIRTH

"When the time came for her to give birth, there were twin boys in her womb. As she was giving birth, one of them put out his hand; so the midwife took a scarlet thread and tied it on his wrist and said, "This one came out first." But when he drew back his hand, his brother came out, and she said, "So this is how you have broken out!" And he was named Perez. Then his brother, who had the scarlet thread on his wrist, came out and he was given the name Zerah" (Gen 38:27-30).

The church has been pregnant since the day the power of the Holy Ghost descended upon her at Pentecost. The power of the Holy Ghost has been incubating diverse gifts and ministries which the sovereign Lord is about to release. It is true that the church has seen the release of diverse gifts, ministries and workings throughout this apostolic age but to the best of it, all these have just been birth pangs. The multiple babies the church has carried in her womb for over two thousand years are about to be brought forth. The preparations that have been going on are in the final stages, and soon the babies will be released.

Unlike before, we are going to witness in a great measure of the release of apostolic and prophetic power. I am not talking of the self-ordained apostles and prophets who fill the pulpits today. It is true that there are God-ordained apostles and prophets in the church today, but these are just in the ratio of about two in a thousand of God's children. It is time for the Lord to release in the field, God-ordained and Holy Ghost-commissioned Apostles and Prophets in a ratio of one to ten who will invade the un-evangelized areas of our world in this last minute before the King returns.

> *The spirit of Perez is about to be released and visions and ministries that are overdue will break out from their hiding places and from the comfort of the womb.*

The spirit of Perez is about to be released and visions and ministries that are overdue will break out from their hiding places and from the comfort of the womb. Many people have carried visions in their spiritual wombs for too long. The Lord is inducing birth pangs for the visions and ministries to break forth.

It has taken the Bridegroom so much to watch over His bride and provide medical care so that her pregnancy is not aborted. The enemy has fought tirelessly over the years to abort this pregnancy because he knows what the multiple babies will do against his works.

Oh, beloved, you who are carrying that pregnant vision, that ministry about to be released, because it is time to give birth you are at a very critical stage. Your vision or your own life is at stake.

It has taken you determination to keep that pregnancy!

It has taken you willingness to carry that vision!
It has taken you patient endurance to watch that pregnancy come to maturity!
It has taken you care, caution for the pregnancy to mature!
In a time like this, you must watch the conditions in which you place that pregnancy. Be careful with what enters fetus. It can deform and destroy it. Keep away from all that can provoke difficult delivery or still birth.

Make Room!

Life begins with a struggle to come out of confinement. It begins with a breaking out for more space and better conditions. It begins with breaking limits and opening closed doors. Some limitations and confinements are for a purpose. The fetus is confined and limited to the womb for a purpose – so as to be nurtured and protected. However a time comes when the fetus must be exposed to the adverse conditions of life. When such a time comes it either breaks free or perishes. It is time for that vision to break free or perish. It is time for that ministry of yours to break free or perish. For any overdue pregnancy, the lives of both the mother and the baby are in great danger.

Life begins with a desperate search for more; more space, more freedom, more oxygen, more food, and more light. Life begins with a risky step into an unknown, uncertain and unexpected domain. It consists of stepping out of a comfort zone into a risky zone. You cannot allow fear to rob you of the possibility of bringing forth that vision. You cannot afford to remain in any unnecessary confinement. Seek for more room because of the baby inside of you. The one who wins is not the one who attempts and shrinks but the one who leaps out in faith. To be a victor there must be a consistent and persistent breaking out of all limitations which are not God-ordained.

Zerah could have been the first but because of fear of the unknown he drew back into the comfort of the womb. Perez took the bold step not minding what was out there. At times daring, most often recklessly daring is the only sure way to break free from limitations and create room for expansion.

Nothing is as awful as when a pregnant woman comes to the time of labor and there is no strength to push out the baby. It is a time of awful distress and agony both to the mother and the baby. There is a very thin line of separation between life and dead for both actors on the scene. As the Bible says,

"… This day is a day of distress and rebuke and disgrace, as when children come to the point of birth and there is no strength to deliver them" (Isa 37:3).

It seems to me that the church is in such a day but the Holy Bridegroom is about to release new strength and power upon His lovely Bride to bring forth the multiple children of visions and ministries that will speed up His return. The purpose of the revival that the Father will bring upon His Son's Bride is to make available all that is needed to bring forth the babies and nurture them to maturity for greatest havoc in the kingdom of the evil one.

And this will be the effect of the soon coming unprecedented outpouring of the Holy Spirit upon the church:

"Before she goes into labor, she gives birth; before the pains come upon her,

she delivers a son. Who has ever heard of such a thing? Who has ever seen such things?

Can a country be born in a day or a nation be brought forth in a moment? Yet no sooner is Zion in labor than she gives birth to her children. Do I bring to the moment of birth and not give delivery?" says the LORD. "Do I close up the womb when I bring to delivery?" says your God. "Rejoice with Jerusalem and be glad for her, all you who love her; rejoice greatly with her, all you who mourn over her. For you will nurse and be satisfied at her comforting breasts; you will drink deeply and delight in her overflowing abundance" (Isa 66:7-11).

> *The Holy Bridegroom is about to release new strength and power upon His lovely Bride to bring forth the multiple children of visions and ministries that will speed up His return.*

- No more struggles for visions and ministries
- No more painful toil with little to show for it
- Rapid growth and maturity of visions and ministries
- A time when there will be more than enough for every vision and ministry
- A time when there will be abundant supplies to every ministry, and an overflow.

The world will soon be running to the church for its needs. I see an overflowing abundance spreading from the church to every sphere of humanity. Mighty rivers of overflowing abundance from Spirit- birthed visions and ministries will soon cover the face of the earth. The glory of the King of the universe is about to invade the earth; O, let it come. Father, let it come, Lord Jesus let it come,

Spirit Divine let it come, so that every other thing will fade and give way.

A Time for Enlargement

In I Chronicles 4:10, Jabez cried out to God for his territory to be enlarged. And God granted his request. It seems as if the church has been contented with the narrow strip of land she has possessed thus far instead of the abundance allotted to her. In her complacency, barrenness and unholy contentment, this is the word of the Lord God Almighty to her.

> *"Sing, O barren woman, you who never bore a child; burst into song, shout for joy, you who were never in labor; because more are the children of the desolate woman than of her who has a husband," says the LORD. "Enlarge the place of your tent, stretch your tent curtains wide, do not hold back; lengthen your cords, strengthen your stakes. For you will spread out to the right and to the left; your descendants will dispossess nations and settle in their desolate cities"* (Isa 54:1-3).

It is time for the barren visions and ministries to burst into song. It is time to shout for joy - Holy Ghost inspired and generated joy, because more are the children to be born in this hour than have ever been born from the day the church came into existence. The Lord is asking you and me to enlarge everything that has to be enlarged. You have to begin from your heart. Enlarge your heart to be able to contain more people. People from races, tribes, cultures, and social backgrounds you had no room for must now find a place in your heart. You must increase your finances to make room for some. You must enlarge your ministry to make room for the lost whom the Spirit shall gather in. You must make room for the sick, the poor, the injured, the wounded, the weak, and the destitute.

You who are contented with your two hundred-seater auditorium had better start making room for a two thousand-seater. You who are contented with a one thousand-seater auditorium should begin to enlarge it to a ten thousand-seater. The Lord says you have got to enlarge and make room for more; more blessings, more insight, more foresight, more wisdom, and more revelations. More, more, more!

CHAPTER FOURTEEN

A TIME FOR THE GLORY TO RETURN

It seems to me, and the evidences are all over, that we the so called Pentecostal and Evangelical people have little power to show in these last days. It is true that there are a few dotted ministries here and there where the glory and the power of the omnipotent God is made manifest. But for the greater part all we hear is Pentecostal and Evangelical noise making.

We have invited people to "power packed services" only for them to come and listen to us preach and sing without results. The people are tired of listening to our loud music, singing and preaching all devoid of Pentecostal power and the glory of the Most High. More and more, our services and programs are becoming entertainment shows.

The Christian life is a life of power from beginning to end. At the beginning we are given power to become children of God (John 1:12). We were saved through the power of God; that blessed Gospel of Christ Jesus our Lord (Romans 1:16). Paul said, "For the kingdom of God is not a matter of talk but of power" (I Corinthians 4:20). But we seem to have made it a matter of talk shows here and there. Sermons filled with words of human wisdom here and there. No doubt the lack of results we see everywhere. We have replaced the power of God with our wisdom.

Paul wrote, "For I resolved to know nothing while I was with you except Jesus Christ crucified. I came to you in weakness and fear, and with much trembling. My message and my preaching were not with wise and persuasive words, but with a demonstration of the Spirit's power, so that your faith might not rest on men's wisdom, but on God's power" (I Corinthians 2:2-5). On the contrary, we the ministers of today seem to have resolved to know everything than life transforming power. We have approached the lost world with the power of the flesh, the power of our appeals, P.A systems, and the media, yet the power of God has been largely absent. Is that not why the greater part of our congregations still knows nothing of Master's transforming power?

I have come to the point where, if a demonstration of God's power will not accompany every message of mine, I better keep my mouth shut. It is no longer time for wise and persuasive gospels but that which carries with it divine power to break mental and spiritual strongholds in the mind and hearts of those listening.

Let us not have the people's faith rest on our wisdom any longer, for it will carry them nowhere. If God's power is demonstrated, the people's faith will rest on His power. And that power is able to carry them through every storm into the divine supernatural realm. Peter said, "His divine power has given us everything we need for life and godliness through our knowledge of him who called us by his own glory and goodness. Through these he has given us his very great and precious promises, so that through them you may participate in the divine nature and escape the corruption in the world caused by evil desires"(2 Peter 1:3-4).

It is through His divine power that we have everything we need. It is through His divine power that we partake of His precious promises. It is through His divine power that we participate in the divine nature. It is time for this power to accompany the preaching of the gospel once again. Like Paul, let us be able to say to those we lead that "For we know, brothers loved by God, that he has chosen you, because our gospel came to you not simply with words, but also with power, with the Holy Spirit and with deep conviction"(I Thessalonians 1:4-5a).

Where is the glory?

In I Samuel 4, we find Israel in the battle front, face to face with their arch enemies – the Philistines. The moral and spiritual bankruptcy of the Israelites made them totally vulnerable to defeat. After suffering serious casualties they resorted to bring in the ark of the covenant of God. They were contented with the form when the actual presence of God had departed. The glory was no longer residing in Shiloh, where the ark was found. Earlier on, "The Lord continued to appear at Shiloh and there He revealed Himself to Samuel through his word" (I Sam 3:21).

If He appeared it meant He was no longer residing there, though the ark was still there. The Israelites who were contented with the shadow instead of the substance thought that, even in their state of moral depravity there could be no difference in power as long as the Ark of the Covenant was there. The very covenant they were transgressing by their own lifestyle.

The Bible says, "Hophni and Phinehas were there with the ark of the covenant of God" (I Sam 4:4^b). It is this same Hophni and Phinehas of which it is written earlier: "Eli's sons were wicked men; they had no regard for the LORD" (I Sam 2:12). They even committed fornication with the women who served at the temple (V 22) and yet carried the ark into battle. This same ark that parted the

Jordan could accomplish nothing when it was carried by these unconverted Priests.

Similarly, although it is true that the gospel is the power of God to bring full salvation for all who believe, its power is greatly diminished when it is proclaimed by those who have not known the working of the cross in their life. The gospel has been rendered void because it has been made an affair of intellectualism.

Intellectualism has taken the gospel captive and made it void of its power to save, heal, and deliver. That is why we find all the gospel talk shows for entertainment and gratification of the intellect. Surely, many people wonder why there is all the shouting and Pentecostal and evangelical noise making. We have given a false impression that the power of God is being demonstrated amongst us when it actually isn't the case.

If we let God's power and glory to return, then the enemy and his human agents who seem to feel very free in our midst will begin to cry out "we're in trouble! ... Woe to us! Who will deliver us from the hand of this mighty God?" Then they will either be converted or flee from the gathering of the saints. For how long, because of the absence of the glory shall we continue to face defeat in the hands of sin, sickness, the world and demons? Is there no power available for us?

There should be no further delay. Let us take away all that has caused the glory to depart from our midst. Let us purge our hearts of every sin and filth. Let us bath ourselves in the blood and purify the temple, making it habitable by His glory. It is time for the glory to return.

The gospel must once again be accompanied everywhere it is proclaimed by the power of the Holy Ghost. Then truly, Satan will be in trouble. His works will be destroyed. His agents will be arrested, stripped of their schemes and devices and brought to allegiance to the King of the universe. It is time we move from Ezekiel chapter ten, where the glory departed from the temple of God to chapter forty-three where the glory returned, then church life will once again be heaven on earth.

> *Intellectualism has taken the gospel captive and made it void of its power to save, heal, and deliver.*

It Is High Time We Opened the Door to the King

In chapter four, we talk of the need to face reality. We saw that we are in the state of the Laodicean church. It should be noted that the King was outside the Church and He said "Here I am! I stand at the door and knock. If anyone hears my voice and opens the door, I will come in and eat with him, and he with me" (Rev 3:20).

We are void of the power and the glory because the King of glory is out. Let us bring Him in to reign in our hearts and churches then He shall bring in His power and the glory for ever and ever. He has been knocking endlessly but we seem to be fast asleep in indulgence, complacently and luxuries from our illicit relationship with a renegade world. It is time we get out of complacently and indulgence and open the door for our darling King to come in and take His place, so that He can wine and dine with us.

It May Cost Us More

"Seek the LORD while he may be found; call on him while he is near" (Isa 55:6).

Now that the King is knocking, it is time we open every door of our heart and life and let Him into every room and compartment.

Let us fling open every door and let His glory fill every room. If we leave any door closed at this time to the King, then it may cost us more to have Him enter some other time. You reading these words please open every door of your heart to the King. Let there be no secret chamber into which He is denied access.

Lay bare your whole life before Him and let Him saturate it with His power and glory. Will you delay any further? There is a time that God can be found and there is a time when He cannot be found. Now that you are reading these words is the time for you. You cannot afford to make any delay. You may delay and open the door at a time He is gone.

> *"I slept but my heart was awake. Listen! My lover is knocking: "Open to me, my sister, my darling,*
> *my dove, my flawless one. My head is drenched with dew, my hair with the dampness of the night." I have taken off my robe--must I put it on again? I have washed my feet--must I soil them again? My lover thrust his hand through the latch-opening; my heart began to pound for him. I arose to open for my lover, and my hands dripped with myrrh, my fingers with flowing myrrh, on the handles of the lock. I opened for my lover, but my lover had left; he was gone. My heart sank at his departure. I looked for him but did not find him. I called him but he did not answer"* (Song of Songs 5:2-6).

She paid a greater price when "the watchmen found me as they made their rounds in the city. They beat me, they bruised me; they took away my cloak, those watchmen of the walls! Outstanding among ten thousand" (v7).

Let Him come in so you can be transformed by the radiance of His face. Let Him come in so that every illegal occupant will fly out through the windows. Let Him in, so that He can make of you all that you were meant to be. May it not be said of you: "when I called, they did not listen; so when they called, I would not listen' says the LORD God Almighty" (Zechariah 7:13).

Let Him in with His life-transforming, destiny fulfilling glory. Let Him saturate your life with His life-preservation aroma. It will preserve, conserve, and reserve you for all that God ordained for you before the foundation of the world. No one filled with the glory ever experiences failure and defeat but they become gateways to wonder-working exploits.

www.ingramcontent.com/pod-product-compliance
Lightning Source LLC
Chambersburg PA
CBHW020139130526
44591CB00030B/148